Chinese Medicine

for everyday living

Chinese Medicine
for everyday living

Penelope Ody

Bounty
Books

First published in 2014 by Bounty Books,
a division of Octopus Publishing Group Ltd
Carmelite House
50 Victoria Embankment
London EC4Y 0DZ
www.octopusbooks.co.uk

An Hachette UK Company
www.hachette.co.uk

Material previously published in *The Chinese Medicine Bible*

This edition reprinted in 2015, 2017

ISBN: 978-0-753728-41-3

A CIP catalogue record for this book is available from the
British Library

NOTE: Printed and bound in China Chinese pictograms are generally transliterated
into English using the pinyin or Wade-Giles systems. These are slightly different: qì in
pinyin, for example, is ch'i in Wade-Giles. The Chinese use different positions of the
tongue in Mandarin to alter the sounds of words giving entirely different meanings
for each apparently similar transliteration: diacritical marks are generally used in
pinyin to guide pronunciation and thus meaning. For simplicity in this book where
Chinese names are given in the text they are usually written in the pinyin form but
without accents and these are only included where there could be confusion. For
clarity where a word used in English implies a Chinese interpretation (as in the
names of the body organs or syndromes), it is given a capital letter.

This book is not intended as an alternative to personal medical advice. The reader
should consult a physician in all matters relating to health and particularly in
respect of any symptoms that may require diagnosis or medical attention. While the
advice and information are believed to be accurate and true at the time of going to
press, neither the author nor the publisher can accept any legal responsibility or
liability for any error or omissions that may have been made.

CONTENTS

INTRODUCTION

Chinese medicine begins with myth – around 5,000 years ago there lived two great emperors, the Yellow, Huang Di, and the Red, Yan Di. The Yellow Emperor taught mankind to weave silk, play musical scales and practise the martial arts while the Red Emperor was the first to cultivate the five grains (millet, rye, sesame and two types of wheat), introducing agriculture to the world and earning the title Divine Farmer or Shen Nong.

Shen Nong was the first to make tea, and he also tasted hundreds of plants and minerals to discover their medicinal properties, so tradition says, because he had a transparent body and could see the effects on himself of the various herbal brews. He is claimed as the author of China's first herbal, the *Shen Nong Ben Cao Jing* (*The Divine Farmer's Herb Classic*), although the book itself was compiled in more recent historic times.

Huang Di, meanwhile, was also helping mankind learn more about medicine; with the help of his physician Qi Bo, he is credited with the *Huang Di Nei Jing Su Wen* (usually abbreviated to *Nei Jing*) — the Yellow Emperor's Classic of Internal Medicine, believed to have been written around 1000 BCE. The *Nei Jing* discusses the nature of *yin* and *yang* as well as the theory of the five elements and their impact on the universe, human health and bodily functions. The book was annotated and expanded many times over the centuries with surviving texts dating from the 14th century CE.

The theories explained in the *Nei Jing* form the focus of this book and are the basis of traditional Chinese herbal medicine as it is still practised today, while the 365 herbs, minerals and animal parts listed in Shen Nong's herbal are among the most important Chinese remedies in current use.

CENTURIES OF PRACTICE

While Chinese medicine began with myth, its practice has been recorded for centuries: around 400 BCE Qin Yueren first described Chinese diagnostic techniques; acupuncture needles have been found in Han Dynasty tombs (206 BCE—CE 220); Tao Honjing in the 6th century CE

Shen Nong, the Divine Father, identified hundreds of herbs.

expanded Shen Nong's list of herbs to 730 remedies; while the great herbalist Li Shi Zhen (1518—1573) published his *Ben Cao Gang Mu* in the 1590s, listing some 1,892 remedies. Over the centuries the traditional theories were gradually expanded, with medical scholars producing detailed texts on everything from treating feverish diseases and epidemics to childhood disorders and skin problems. There was also a focus on acupuncture.

While the formalized theories and remedies credited to Huang Di and Shen Nong were familiar to the affluent ruling classes of Chinese society, most people depended on folk medicine and itinerant physicians. This meant that healthcare in remote regions remained extremely basic for many centuries.

All this began to change in the 18th century, however, with the arrival of European missionaries and traders. Western-style dissections of corpses — previously banned — demonstrated the true function of the various organs. Chinese doctors began to travel abroad to study this new medicine with the first student, Huang Kuan, arriving at Edinburgh's noted medical school in the 1850s.

By the beginning of the 20th century China had its own colleges teaching Western medicine and the traditional techniques of old were largely dismissed as unscientific.

TRADITIONAL MEDICINE IN A MODERN AGE

Perhaps the most famous of China's Western-style doctors was Sun Yat-sen (1866—1925), who led the revolution that overthrew the last Qing emperor in 1911. Sun had studied medicine in Guangzhou (Canton) and Hong Kong and practised at a Macao hospital before taking to politics. He was a keen advocate of Western medicine, and the new Nationalist government imposed restrictions on the traditional techniques by banning new colleges and strictly controlling practice. The strategy met with considerable resistance and compromise became inevitable; research into Chinese remedies was undertaken to demonstrate their efficacy in scientific terms, and attempts were made to merge Western and traditional Chinese medical theories.

Under Mao Zedong in the 1950s, new traditional Chinese medicine colleges were established in Shanghai, Liaoning, Zhejiang, and Henan, along with many factories producing pills, powders and tonics based on traditional prescriptions.

Today, traditional Chinese medicine is available throughout China, as is our familiar Western medicine, with patients able to choose treatments from either discipline — or indeed, to opt for the many regional folk cures which still survive.

Sun Yat-sen was a western-trained doctor who frowned on traditional medicine.

THE THEORY OF CHINESE MEDICINE

THE NATURAL WORLD
AND THE FIVE-ELEMENT THEORY

Traditional Chinese medicine developed from a very different view of the world to that which we hold today. Some ancient Greek philosophers argued that everything was composed of four core elements – earth, air, fire and water – but the Chinese imagined a world derived from five processes: wood (*mu*), fire (*huo*), earth (*tu*), metal (*jin*) and water (*shui*) known collectively as *wuxing* or *wu xing* (usually translated as movements or elements).

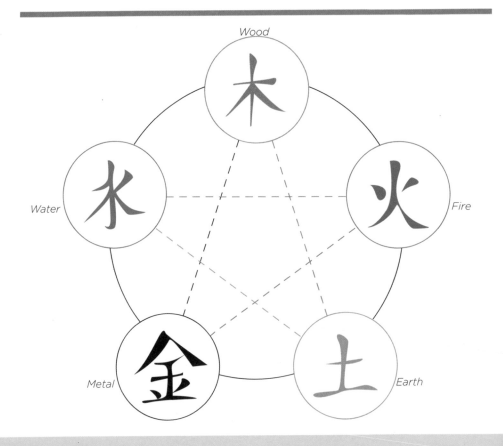

The earth element is associated with the change from one season to the next.

Unlike the Western elements these movements are not fixed substances but are more active. Wood, for example, is associated with growing, while fire is transforming.

The five elements are closely related and reflect the seasonal changes those early thinkers saw in the world around them. Winter rains (water), gave rise to new growth in spring (wood), which in turn would be burnt in the scorching heat of a central Asian summer (fire), to create ashes (earth), from which metal ores could be extracted, metal in its turn is cold causing the water vapour in warm air to appear as condensation.

Each element therefore gives rise to the next in the cycle – traditionally described as a mother-son relationship – so water is seen as the mother of wood while metal gives birth to wood. The strength or weakness of each element also affects that of its neighbours: too little water and the green shoots in spring will not appear, too little fire and there will be no ashes to strengthen earth, and so on. In the reverse direction there are also controlling influences: wood will absorb water, and water can rust metal, metal can break up earth, which will smother fire, while fire burns wood.

CONTROLS AND RESTRAINTS

Each element also exerts control over others elsewhere in the cycle: water, obviously, can put out fire while fire will melt metal, metal can chop wood while wood in the form of roots can divide and move earth, while earth, in its turn, will muddy water. There are reverse restraints, too, since wood will absorb water, which also rusts metal, while metal breaks up earth, which can smother fire and fire can, of course burn wood.

Having created a world view in which everything is linked to five core elements the Chinese then extended the model to take in every aspect of life: five seasons, five directions, five colours, five tastes, five sounds, and so on.

They also identified five *zang* or solid organs in the body and five *fu* or hollow organs. These organs are conceptual and bear little relation to accepted anatomy and physiology. The relationship between these organs is also the same as that between the elements so the Liver is seen as the mother of the Heart, while the Kidneys are the mother of the Liver. Equally the Heart (fire) will control the Lungs (metal) while Kidneys (water) can control the Heart (fire). Illness in one organ can thus be traced to a weakness or over-controlling action by a related organ. If water is weak, for example, it will fail to control fire, which becomes over-exuberant and attacks metal; or in organ terms, weak Kidneys fail to control the Heart, which then damages the Lungs, so a respiratory disorder such as asthma may in some cases be treated with kidney tonics.

Other aspects of the five-element relationships also affect health and diagnosis: a craving for or dislike of sour tastes may suggest Liver imbalance or excessive grief may lead to Lung weakness.

Wood represents new growth.

FIVE ELEMENTS CONNECTIONS

	Wood	Fire	Earth	Metal	Water
Direction	East	South	Centre	West	North
Colour	Green	Red	Yellow	White	Black
Season	Spring	Summer	Late Summer	Autumn	Winter
Climate	Wind	Hot	Dampness	Dryness	Cold
Solid or zang organs	Liver	Heart	Spleen	Lung	Kidney
Hollow or fu organs	Gall bladder	Small intestine	Stomach	Large intestine	Urinary bladder
Sense organs/ openings	Eyes/sight	Tongue/ speech	Mouth/taste	Nose/smell	Ears/hearing
Emotion	Anger	Joy/fright	Worry	Sadness/grief	Fear
Taste	Sour	Bitter	Sweet/acrid	Pungent	Salty
Tissues	Tendon/ nails	Blood vessels Complexion	Muscles/lips	Skin/body hair	Bone/head hair
Sound	Shouting	Laughing	Singing	Weeping	Groaning
Smell	Rancid	Burnt	Fragrant	Rotten	Putrid
Secretions	Tears	Sweat	Saliva	Mucus	Urine
Spiritual aspects	Soul (*hun*)	Spirit (*shen*)	Intention (*yi*)	Vitality (*po*)	Determination (zhi)
Fingers	Index	Thumb	Middle	Ring	Little
Lifecycle	Birth	Youth	Adulthood	Old age	Death

OPPOSITES IN EQUILIBRIUM
— YIN AND YANG

The concept of *yin* and *yang* is central to Chinese medical theory and describes how opposing forces can be inter-connected and inter-dependent while present in all things. One common analogy is a mountain — one side bathed in bright sunlight and the other in deep shadow creating two very different environments within one totality. This single entity containing two opposing forces is characterized by the traditional Taoist *taijitu* diagram — *taijitu* means 'diagram of ultimate power'.

Yang is often described in the West as representing masculine energies while *yin* is seen as softer and more feminine, but this is a vast over-simplification. *Yin-yang* is not so much an actual entity or force but, like the five elements in the five-element model, it represents processes rather than actual things. It is a more dynamic interaction that is always present and changing rather than an absolute: above/below; outside/inside; strong/weak; dry/damp; hot/cold and so on. *Yang* can be represented by fire: upward moving, bright, warm, active, exciting; while *yin* is water: sinking downwards, dim, cold, passive, inhibiting. Both are, however, always present: hot summer may be more *yang* in character but *yin* is still present in cooler nights while winter is *yin* but still contains some sunny *yang* days.

While *yin* and *yang* are opposites and sometimes said to be in dynamic equilibrium, they are also held in balance: one cannot exist without the other and if the balance is tilted then there can be problems. Within Chinese medicine body parts and functions are seen as more or less *yin* or *yang* although all contain aspects of both.

Substances – passive, unchanging – are seen as more *yin*, while functions – active, changing – are more *yang*. The solid *zang* organs that are associated with storage are thus more *yin* in character, while the hollow *fu* organs that have functions associated with transforming are therefore *yang*. The outside of the body is more *yang* while the inside is more *yin*; the upper half more *yang*, the lower parts more *yin*. Thus the

The Taoist bagua *symbol shows the* taijitu *surrounded by the eight trigrams representing the fundamental principles of reality.*

CHARACTERISTICS OF YIN AND YANG

Yin	Yang
Water	Fire
Dark	Light
Cold	Hot
Passive	Active
Inside	Outside
Slow	Rapid
Right	Left
Dim	Bright
Downwards	Upwards
Substance	Function
Matter	Energy

Lungs – *zang* and *yin* – will be slightly more *yang* in character than the Kidneys (also *zang* and *yin*) because they are in the upper part of the body (*yang*) while the Kidneys are lower down (*yin*).

MAINTAINING BALANCE

Within the body, the relationship between *yin* and *yang* is constantly changing; sitting indoors, quietly reading a book sees us in a more *yin* mode, while energetically digging the garden on a sunny afternoon is definitely a *yang*-promoting activity.

In health these changes are normal and easily managed; however, in illness or disease the mutual restraint of the opposing forces can

Calm, quiet, indoor activities are considered yin.

become out of control leading to serious imbalance. Identifying these imbalances is an important aspect of Chinese diagnostics with four possible scenarios for the imbalance. Two scenarios involve over-activity leading to Excess disorders and two involve under-activity, leading to Deficiency syndromes.

Excess and deficiency

If *yin* is in excess then it can damage *yang* and cause Cold and Excess disorders, while if *yang* is over-active it can lead to Hot and Excess syndromes. If *yin* is weak then *yang* is in apparent excess but this is actually a *yin* Deficiency problem rather than one of surplus *yang* and the result is a Hot and Deficiency syndrome, while if the reverse is true then there is a Cold and Deficiency problem.

In addition, there may be cases in which both *yin* and *yang* are Deficient or where they are both in Excess, giving rise to two further possibilities for imbalance.

Obviously in diagnosis it is essential to reach the right conclusion, since different treatments will apply. Apparent Cold symptoms could be due to weak *yang* – Cold and Deficiency – or they could result from over-active *yin* (Cold and Excess). In the first case treatment would be focused on strengthening *yang*, and in the second on controlling over-exuberant *yin*. However, if the wrong treatment was given, for example, reducing *yin* in a Deficiency disorder, then the syndrome could progress to general *yin-yang* weakness and even greater debility.

Vigorous outdoor activities are considered yang.

ZANG ORGANS

To the ancient Chinese the body contained five *zang* or solid organs – Heart, Liver, Spleen, Lung and Kidneys. These were said to resemble the solidness of the Earth and were associated with storage so are more *yin* in character. It is important to remember that these organs are not the same as our modern anatomical and physiological concepts: they embrace related systems and include spiritual and emotional aspects as well as physical entities.

The *zang* organs each have an associated hollow organ – the *fu* organs – which are involved with transformation and activity, so are more *yang* in character. The *zang* and *fu* organs are linked by meridians or acupuncture channels (see pages 30–34). Each organ also has an associated fundamental substance such as Blood or *qi* (which is translated as life-force or breath). All these connections relate to the five-element model).

THE HEART

The Heart (*xin*) is generally regarded as the most important or 'emperor' of the *zang* organs and is associated with thought and intellect. This is consistent with other ancient medical traditions such as Ayurveda in India where the heart is closely linked to spiritual and emotional activity.

Rather than regarding the heart as a mechanical pump, the Chinese maintain that blood flows through the arteries and veins because of the power of Heart *qi*. When this is strong and abundant it can be felt as a smooth and forceful pulse; if Heart *qi* is weak then so too is the pulse.

Mind and spirit

Mental activity also comes under the Heart's dominion: in Chinese terminology this activity includes a wide range of life processes not just perception and thought. In contrast, the brain is simply regarded as a place to receive and store impressions. In Chinese the word for Heart and mind – *xin* – is the same.

The Heart is also said to store the Spirit (*shen*), which is sometimes equated with awareness. Several herbal remedies are also described as calming the Spirit and are used to ease mental and emotional upsets that can be linked to a range of Heart disorders.

Because of the very strong link between the blood vessels and the Heart, the condition of the Heart is said to be seen in a person's complexion, where a glowing, healthy-looking complexion signifies a similarly healthy Heart while a pale, dull face suggests that there are some weakness.

Chinese theory also maintains that we can taste foods because the tongue is supplied with Heart *qi* and is the body opening of the Heart.

HEART FUNCTION

The Heart is believed to control all life processes and coordinates the activities of all the other *zang-fu* organs. In addition it:

- governs the Blood circulation and vessels
- controls mental activities
- stores the Spirit
- is seen in the condition of the complexion
- is linked to the tongue.

Performing tai chi contributes to a state of mental clarity.

THE LIVER

The Liver (*gan*) is sometimes referred to as the 'general' of the *zang* organs and works with the Heart to control the Blood supply. The ancient Chinese believed that Blood travelled through the vessels when the body was active but during rest it was stored in the Liver, so it was called the 'Reservoir of Blood'. This association of the Liver with Blood is why in Chinese theory the Liver is closely linked to the menstrual cycle.

In traditional Chinese medicine the Liver is said to favour a smooth flow of *qi* and has an aversion to stagnancy. A smooth *qi* flow helps to regulate emotional activities, while stagnation or obstruction leads to moodiness, anger and depression. It also ensures normal digestive function: for the Spleen and Stomach to function properly a smooth flow of *qi* is essential, with irregularity causing dysfunction such as indigestion or jaundice. A smooth *qi* flow from the Liver is also important for the Triple Burner (*san jiao* see page 28–29) – a mysterious concept to Westerners but important for controlling body fluids.

In traditional Chinese theory it is believed that the Spirit resides in the Heart during the day and the Liver at night when we sleep, when its state can be assessed by dreams, which is why the Liver is said to 'store the Soul'. Spirit itself divides further into *po* – the animal or physical soul that lives in the Lung and controls physical energies; and *hun* – a more ethereal or spiritual aspect of soul that is stored in the Liver and that controls both conscious and unconscious thought.

The Liver also controls the tendons so aching knees, where there are a great many tendons, can suggest a Liver imbalance. The nails are believed to indicate the state of Liver energies and health with strong, pink nails implying a strong Liver. In conventional medicine pale fingernails often indicate iron-deficient anaemia, whereas the Chinese see this as evidence of a weakened Liver and thus failure to store Blood efficiently. The Liver's role in storing Blood is also said to be one reason why it is linked to the eyes with Deficient Liver Blood leading to poor vision or night blindness; dry eyes and conjunctivitis are similarly linked to weaknesses in the Liver.

LIVER FUNCTION

The Liver is said to:

- store Blood
- regulate the flow of *qi*
- store the Soul
- control the tendons
- it can also be seen in the nails and is linked to the eyes.

The function of the spleen is closely related to digestion.

THE SPLEEN

In Western medicine the Spleen (*pi*) filters old red blood cells from our blood and stores blood, and is part of the immune system. In Chinese theory, the Spleen (*pi*) is mainly concerned with digestive function and is responsible for the assimilation and distribution of nutrients and water in the body.

If the Spleen is working well, then 'food essence' will be efficiently distributed to the Lungs and Heart, from where it is sent to the rest of the body so that muscles and tissues will be well-formed. The Spleen plays a similar role in managing water distribution through the body, extracting it from food and drink and sending it to the Lungs, Heart and Urinary Bladder. When Spleen *qi* is strong, Blood is kept within the blood vessels, if *qi* is weak then the Blood can escape to form haemorrhages or subcutaneous bleeding.

Will power

Just as the Heart and Liver have a spiritual dimension so too does the Spleen, storing *yi*, which is intention or will power and helps us to make necessary changes in our lives. Spleen weakness or damage can lead to mental confusion, indecisiveness or poor memory.

The mouth is also linked to the Spleen – not only is it connected through the muscles, but it is the primary source of the food that the Spleen processes. Its body opening is the lips: full, red, lustrous lips suggest that nutrients are being processed and distributed well, while thin, pale lips and poor appetite suggest Spleen malfunction.

SPLEEN FUNCTION

The Spleen is said to:

- control digestion
- control the limbs and flesh
- keep Blood in the blood vessels
- store intention or determination
- be linked to the mouth and reflected in the lips.

THE LUNG

The Lung (*fei*) is the 'prime minister', of the *zang* organs, managing air and water within the body and, importantly, controlling *qi* flow.

In Chinese theory, as indeed with yoga practices from India, breath is linked to vital energy so it is understandable that the ancients linked the Lung to the flow of *qi*. The Lung is especially associated with *wei qi*, a form of defence energy that can be equated with the immune system. Lung *qi* is believed to disperse *wei qi* and Body Fluids to help warm and nourish the skin and muscles. The skin is especially associated with the Lung, with the sweat pores known in Chinese medicine as the 'portal of energy': production of sweat is under the control of the *wei qi*.

Lung *qi* has a downward direction so it ensures that water and body fluids travel throughout the body and down to the urinary bladder for excretion. Any weakness in Lung *qi* can thus lead to oedema or fluid retention.

Animal soul

The Lung also stores an aspect of soul – *po*, the animal soul that manifests as vitality. Sorrow and anxiety can damage this vitality and cause stagnation of Lung *qi* leading to depression and dejection. As one would expect, the nose is the body opening of the Lung with the sense of smell also dependent on Lung *qi*.

THE KIDNEY

As one might expect the Chinese believe that Kidney (*shen*) is responsible for regulating water in the body. An equally important role, however, is to store the vital essence or *jing* – one of the five fundamental substances and the source of living organisms. The Kidney also promotes growth and development of the body and plays an important role in reproduction.

The condition of the Kidney can be seen in the head hair and it is linked to the ears and genitals.

In Chinese theory the Kidney has an important role to play in water metabolism by helping the Lung to co-ordinate respiration by directing the *qi* downwards. Strong Kidney *qi* leads to even, regular breathing while weak Kidney *qi* impairs inhalation leading to 'Deficiency-type' asthma.

Water metabolism is also associated with Body Fluids and the Kidney is responsible for sending clear Fluids upwards to circulate in the tissues while turbid Fluids are transformed into sweat and urine for excretion.

The vital essence (see pages 38–40) stored in the Kidney has many functions including the creation of bone marrow, both that found in the large bones of the body and a 'spinal marrow' believed to fill the spinal chord and brain.

Determination or will (*zhi*) is also stored in the Kidney: strong Kidney *qi* therefore leads to good memory, vigour, wisdom and well-developed skills. If Kidney *qi* is weak then the memory is poor, spirits are low and there is a lack of aspiration. Meridians link the Kidney to the ears, genitals and anus so it is also responsible for hearing, reproduction and excretion. Kidney energy declines with age so signs of ageing – such as balding head hair, and hearing loss – are also linked to Kidney weakness.

FU ORGANS

The *fu* or hollow organs are associated with transformation rather than storage so are thus more *yang* in character than the *zang* organs. One of the *fu* organs is linked to each of the *zang* organ with a sixth – the Triple Burner – a more nebulous entity.

THE SMALL INTESTINE

The Small Intestine (*xiao chang*) forms a *zang-fu* pair with the Heart and is said to have the function of 'receiving and containing' water and food which has been digested in the Stomach. It 'differentiates the usable from the unusable' sorting the usable materials – described as 'clear' – that are eventually transported as nutrients or 'food essence' to other parts of the body while the unusable or turbid are sent onwards as solid wastes to the Large Intestine or as liquid to the Kidney and Urinary Bladder for excretion. Although the terminology may be different the Small Intestine's function is thus much as one would expect from conventional Western physiology.

THE GALL BLADDER

In Western medicine a key function of the gall bladder is to store around 50 ml (2 fl oz) of bile produced by the liver: this is then released to help digest fats. In Chinese theory bile is seen instead as surplus Liver *qi* so plays a part in promoting the smooth flow of *qi* and Blood. The Gall Bladder (*dan*) is also associated with decisiveness, activity and decision-making; in contrast weak Gall Bladder energy can lead to dithering and lack of determination.

THE STOMACH

The Stomach (*wei*) forms a *zang-fu* pair with the Spleen and is primarily involved in taking in and transforming food into chyme, the semi-fluid mass of part-digested food that the stomach sends onwards to the intestines. In Chinese theory, the efficiency of this onward movement is related to the strength of the Stomach *qi* so the vigour of all the *zang-fu* organs depends on the abundance of Stomach *qi*. The Stomach's activity complements that of the Spleen:

The Stomach, as in Western anatomy, plays a major role in digesting food.

Small Intestine is transformed into solid waste for excretion and water which is reabsorbed. These functions mirror the Western understanding.

THE URINARY BLADDER

The Urinary Bladder (*pang guang*) is linked to the Kidney and stores and excretes urine. In Chinese theory, the Kidney separates clear and turbid Fluids and the Urinary Bladder removes the unusable turbid Fluids from the body. Urinary function is said to be controlled by Kidney *yang* so if this is weak there may be increased frequency of urination or a need to urinate more often at night. The Chinese say that when Kidney energy is strong, there is no need for frequent urination.

THE TRIPLE BURNER

The sixth *fu* organ is the Triple Burner (*san jiao*) which is a concept dating back to the *Yellow Emperor's Classic of Internal Medicine* (at least 1000 BCE). It attempts to describe the digestive function and the separation of clear from turbid Fluid. It is the basis and controller for the circulation of Body Fluids and occupies the entire torso – from the base of the tongue to the anus.

The Upper Burner or *shang jiao* (from tongue to diaphragm) is linked to the function of Heart and Lung, and

In Chinese theory, poor Kidney energy is associated with the need to urinate with greater frequency.

the Spleen maintains the upward flow of *qi*, while the Stomach sends digested food downwards. The Spleen is involved in the upwards transportation of water so is said to be clear with an aversion to Dampness, while the Stomach is turbid so prefers Dampness.

THE LARGE INTESTINE

The Large Intestine (*da chang*) is linked to the Lung and is where the unusable or turbid material from the include transmitting *qi* and nutrients, warming the body, nourishing the skin and spreading the defence energy or *wei qi*.

The Middle Burner or *zhong jiao* (from diaphragm to navel) reflects the functions of the Spleen and Stomach and is mainly concerned with digesting foods, absorbing and transporting nutrients, and producing various Body Fluids.

The Lower Burner or *xia jiao* (from navel to anus) reflects the function of the Kidney, Large Intestine, Small Intestine and Urinary Bladder in separating clear and turbid Fluids and managing excretion. The Liver is also associated with the lower *jiao*, with the smooth flow of Liver *qi* ensuring orderly functioning of the *san jiao*.

The *san jiao* is sometimes paired with the Pericardium which can be defined as a sixth *zang* organ although the classic Chinese texts tend to see this Pericardium-Triple Burner pairing as a subset of the Small Intestine.

Healthy pink nails are said to indicate strong Liver energy.

MERIDIANS: THE CHANNEL SYSTEM

Alongside the *zang-fu* organs, traditional Chinese anatomy also comprises the Channel system – a network of pathways through the body that link the organs and distribute *qi* and other fundamental substances. Keeping these intangible routes, sometimes called meridians, clear of obstructions is vital.

In the West these Channels have become known through acupuncture treatments, with needles used at specific points to stimulate or ease the flow of *qi*. In Chinese theory, however, they have a wider role: herbs are often defined in terms of the meridians they affect while numerous disease syndromes are connected to various Channel afflictions. The concept involves picturing the body as three concentric cylinders. The outer cylinder is home to the flesh and joints, the middle cylinder is where the principal or primary channels run and the innermost cylinder houses the *zang-fu* organs.

The 12 primary Channels (*jing mai*) are linked to the *zang-fu* organs; six of these Channels are *yang* and six are *yin*. They form six pairs with those associated on the front of the limbs known as *taiyin* and *yangming*, those on the back of the limbs as *shaoyin* and *taiyang* and those mid-way known as *jueyin* and *shaoyang*.

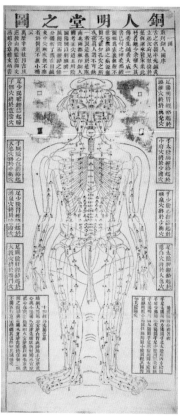

Many health problems are associated with disharmonies within the 12 Channels.

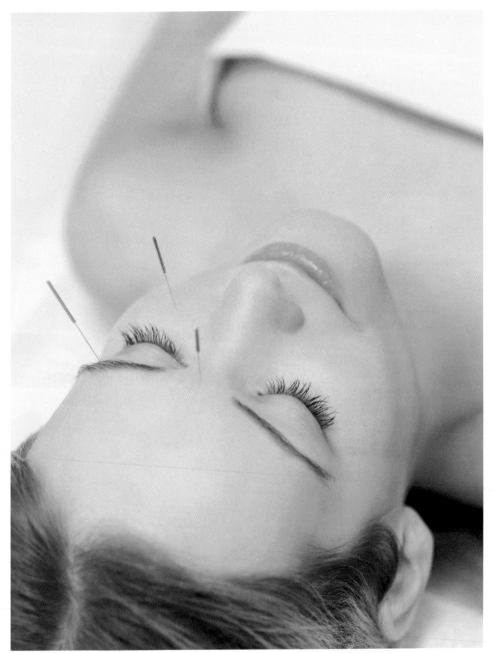

Acupuncture has been used in China since the days of the Yellow Emperor.

12 MAIN CHANNELS
AND ASSOCIATED HEALTH PROBLEMS

Affected organ	Meridian	Typical signs of disharmony
Heart	Hand *shaoyin*	Heart pain, palpitations, insomnia, night sweats
Small intestine	Hand *taiyang*	Deafness, lower abdominal pain and distention
Liver	Foot *jueyin*	Low back or abdominal pain, mental disturbances, hiccups
Bladder	Foot *shaoyang*	Headaches, blurred vision, shoulder pain
Spleen	Foot *taiyin*	Flatulence, vomiting, upper abdominal pain
Stomach	Foot *yangming*	Abdominal bloating, vomiting, abdominal pain
Lung	Hand *taiyin*	Coughs, asthma, chest pain
Large intestine	Hand *yangming*	Toothache, sore throat, neck pain
Kidney	Foot *shaoyin*	Impotence, weakness in the lower limbs, increased frequency of urination
Urinary bladder	Foot *taiyang*	Urinary retention, nasal catarrh, headache, back pain
Pericardium	Hand *jueyin*	Heart pain, poor concentration, palpitations
San jiao	Hand *shaoyang*	Abdominal bloating, deafness, tinnitus, urinary dysfunction

SECONDARY CHANNELS

Eight secondary Channels (*qi jing ba mai*) help communications between pairs of primary Channels to ensure a steady flow of *qi* and Blood. The two most important are the Governing Vessel (*du mai*) and the Conception Vessel (*ren mai*). The *du mai* runs from the anus, up the spine, across the crown of the head and ends inside the upper lip; it governs the *yang* Channels. The *ren mai* governs the *yin* Channels and is closely associated with pregnancy; it runs up the front of the body from the pelvis to the inside of the lower lip.

The other six Channels are the:

- Penetrating Vessel (*chong mai*), which communicates with the main Channels

- Girdle Vessel (*dai mai*), which runs around the waist like a belt and binds all the Channels together

- *Yin* Heel (*yin qiao jing*) associated with excess sleep

- *Yang* Heel (*yang qiao jing*) associated with insomnia

- *Yin* Tie (*yin wie jing*) ties together the *yin* channels, connecting and regulating them

- *Yang* Tie (*yang wei jing*) ties the *yang* Channels together.

Distinct channels

In addition, there are 12 distinct Channels (*bei jing*), that improve communications between *yin* and *yang* Channels and co-ordinate the exterior and the interior of the body, and 15 connecting Channels that are also involved in communication: 13 of these are linked to the primary Channels (the Spleen meridian has two) and two are associated with the *ren mai* and *du mai*.

Tendon-muscle channels

There are 12 tendon-muscle channels located in the superficial tissues and influence how *qi* flows in the muscles rather than the internal organs.

Collateral channels

Finally there are countless small collateral Channels throughout the body that run on the surface and help *qi* and Blood to circulate between the interior and exterior Channels.

ACUPUNCTURE POINTS

On each Channel are a number of points where *qi* is carried to the surface and where acupuncture or other treatments can help to regulate the flow of both *qi* and Blood. There are some 361 points on the 14 main channels, with perhaps 2,000 or more points in total on all Channels and collaterals together, although only around 150 are regularly used in acupuncture treatments.

FUNDAMENTAL SUBSTANCES

Along with the five *zang* and five *fu* organs, the Chinese five-element model also identifies five fundamental substances: *qi, jing, xue, jin-ye* and *shen* – vital life materials on which our health and vitality depends.

Kong qi *is derived from the air we breathe. It is one of the three sources of* qi *in the body.*

VITAL ENERGY

Of the five substances, *qi* is perhaps the most familiar: a concept of essential energy that sits comfortably with the traditional Western notion of a vital life force. *Qi* is, however, far more complex, with some 32 different types of *qi* identified in numerous texts. As a whole, the body's *qi* is generally described as upright (*zheng*) or true (*zhen*), which is a sort of undifferentiated *qi* not associated with specific organs or functions. This *qi* has three possible origins:

- Primordial or prenatal (*yuan qi*) is the *qi* we are born with and derives from our parents

- Grain *qi* (*gu qi*) derived from the food we eat

- Nature or air *qi* (*kong qi*) extracted from the air we breathe.

Zheng or *zhen qi* (referred to just as *qi*) is made from the mingling of these three different types of *qi* and has five major functions covering: movement; protection; transformation of food; warmth; and retention of the body's substances and organs.

Qi is said to be in constant motion and in normal health these movements flow steadily and harmoniously through the meridians. If there is insufficient *qi* or some sort of obstruction then *qi* becomes disordered and ill health follows. In health there is a regular rhythm to this *qi* flow and disharmonies can be identified by the times at which they occur. Waking regularly in the early hours, for example, could suggest some obstruction in energy flow from Liver to Lung.

As well as flowing through the channels, normal *qi* also provides

IDENTIFYING DISHARMONIES

Time	Meridians
3–5 am	Lung
5–7 am	Large Intestine
7–9 am	Stomach
9–11 am	Spleen
11 am–1 pm	Heart
1–3 pm	Small Intestine
3–5 pm	Urinary Bladder
5–7 pm	Kidney
7–9 pm	Pericardium
9–11 pm	*San jiao*
11 pm–1 am	Gall Bladder
1–3 am	Liver

each of the *zang-fu* organs with their own specific *qi* relevant to its particular functions. Other important types include *wei qi* or protective *qi*. This is usually regarded as an aspect of the normal *zheng qi* although it is sometimes described as also derived from grain *qi*.

The *wei qi* can be thought of as an aspect of the immune system defending the body from external attack. The *wei qi* travels on the surface and exterior parts of the body in skin and muscle where it also regulates body temperature and sweating.

This circulation is largely a daytime phenomenon with the *wei qi* travelling up the spine, across the head in the morning, down the front of the body during the afternoon to reach the lower spine at night, where it retreats back into the body. Because of this the time of onset of an external disorder is significant in Chinese medicine.

Pectoral qi and nourishing qi

While normal *qi* is derived from primordial *qi*, grain *qi* and nature *qi*, the grain *qi* and nature *qi* also combine to produce pectoral *qi* (*zong qi*). This is stored in the chest and its main function is to control the rhythms of respiration and heartbeat making it responsible for the movement of the Blood, the voice, and the strength and regularity of breathing and heartbeat.

Nourishing *qi* (*ying qi*) is largely produced from grain *qi*, which is collected and transformed by the Spleen. This form of energy transforms some of the food we eat into Blood, which carries these nutrients to all parts of the body.

While there are many different types of *qi* there are two primary disharmonies that can afflict it and therefore lead to ill health: Deficient (*qi xu*), which manifests as various weaknesses; and Stagnant (*qi zhi*) where the flow is impaired interrupting normal function of the affected organs. In Western terms, health problems associated with the physiological dysfunction of any particular organ would, in Chinese theory, be associated with *qi* problems.

BLOOD

While *xue* is generally translated as Blood in Chinese theory, it indicates a substance with rather more functions than simply carrying oxygen and nutrients to the tissues. *Xue* is also seen as essential for mental activities and circulates not just in the blood vessels, but also in the meridians.

Blood, like post-natal *jing*, is produced from food. The Stomach and Spleen are believed to process the food leading to production of a pure substance, which is then carried by the Spleen *qi* to the Lungs. In the

If Blood (xue) and qi are strong, then a person will be clear-thinking and vigorous.

process this substance begins its conversion into Blood – a process completed by the addition of air in the Lungs. This Blood or *xue* is then propelled through the body by the Heart *qi*. *Qi* – active and therefore *yang* in character – is thus very important for creating and moving Blood, which is liquid and thus *yin* in nature. If *xue* and *qi* are strong then the person will be clear-thinking and vigorous – if not they may lack energy and concentration. *Xue* is particularly associated with three of the *zang* organs: the Heart, the Liver, and the Spleen.

Blood disorders

Health problems associated with Blood fall into two main categories: Deficient Blood (*xue xu*); and Congealed or Stagnant Blood (*xue yu*). Blood may be Deficient throughout the body – typified by pallor, lethargy, dizziness and dry skin. In Chinese theory this would be treated by a herb such as *dang gui* (Chinese angelica), said to nourish the Blood. Alternatively Blood may be Deficient from a specific organ – if the Heart was affected, for example, then there could be irregular heart beat or palpitations.

Stagnant Blood is caused when it is obstructed and no longer flows smoothly through the vessels or the meridians. This may be characterized by sharp stabbing pains and swelling or tumours.

VITAL ESSENCE

Jing can be translated as 'essence' and is the most important of the fundamental substances as it underpins all organic life. Vital essence is stored in the Kidney and derives from two sources: congenital essence (*xian tian zhi jing*); and acquired or post-natal essence (*hiu tian zhi jing*).

Congenital essence

The congenital essence, also known as 'before heaven', is inherited from one's parents: it is unique, is with us from conception, and is responsible for our growth, make-up and constitution. It controls reproduction and creativity. Reproductive problems, such as infertility, impotence, or repeated miscarriages, can all be associated in Chinese medicine with weakness of *jing*.

Congenital essence is also fixed; it cannot be expanded or increased and runs down gradually throughout our lifetime. Its loss is associated with the physical signs of ageing, such as greying hair, deafness, increased

Congenital essence is with us from birth and is inherited from our parents.

urination – all of which are linked in the five-element model to the Kidney and water element.

Post-natal essence

This essence is produced by the Spleen from the purified components in our food and water and is known as 'after heaven'. This essence can help strengthen the vitality of the congenital essence and can itself be improved by good diet and lifestyle. Unlike the fixed 'before heaven' component, this part of the total *jing* can be replenished and can help to compensate for any weaknesses in the inherited congenital *jing*.

In women the run-down in congenital essence is also marked by the start of the menopause, which in Chinese medicine is often treated with Kidney tonics. The original *Yellow Emperor's Classic of Internal Medicine* (the *Nei Jing*) refers to women's lives as occurring in periods of seven years with puberty at age 14, wisdom teeth at 21, and a peak in strength and vitality at 28. By 49 '...the gates of menstruation are no longer open; her body deteriorates and she is no longer able to bear children'.

With men, according to the *Nei Jing*, the life pattern is based on eight-year periods with the final *jing* run-down starting at 56 years of age, when '... his secretion of semen is exhausted, his vitality diminishes, his kidneys deteriorate and his physical strength reaches its end'.

In Chinese theory a woman's reproductive life ends at 49.

While *qi* is associated with movement, *jing* is less dynamic, associated more with inner growth and ultimate decline. It is linked to creativity with excessive creative activity rapidly exhausting the limited supply of congenital *jing*.

As the vital underpinning for organic life, *jing* can also feed some of the other fundamental substances that are said to nuture *xue* (Blood) and *qi* when need be. *Qi* can therefore go some way to help energizing the Spleen so encouraging production

BODY FLUIDS

Jin-ye refers to clear (*jin*) and turbid (*ye*) body fluids and covers all the liquids in the body other than Blood: the category thus includes sweat, urine, saliva, tears, mucus and gastric juices. These body fluids are derived from food and water and converted by the Stomach and Spleen into *jin* and *ye*. Their function is to moisten, lubricate and nourish the body with the heavier, turbid fluids supporting the inner parts of the body and the lighter, clear fluids focused more on the exterior of the body.

Like Blood, the body fluids are *yin* in nature and any disharmonies manifest as dryness as well as forming part of more general *yin* problems. The clear fluids are also involved in the production of Blood so *jin-ye* weakness can also lead to Deficient Blood problems. The *jin-ye* circulate in the body and come under the control of the Spleen, Lungs and Kidneys: weaknesses in these organs can also contribute to Deficient Fluid syndromes.

SPIRIT

If *jing* represents our physical nature and the source of life and *qi* our life force, energy and our ability to move and be active, then *shen* is our spiritual aspect and the vitality of consciousness behind both *jing* and *qi*. The word is generally translated

In traditional Chinese theory, men reach old age at 56 when 'kidneys deteriorate and physical strength reaches its end'.

of post-natal essence. *Jing* is also associated with the production of bone marrow, which ancient Chinese theory also equates with the brain. Brain damage or weaknesses in memory and concentration are also thus associated with *jing* Deficiency and may be treated with strengthening Kidney tonics. If *qi* is the energetic life force that dictates our vitality and activity, then *jing* also functions as the physical bedrock that underlies our basic strength and reproduction.

as 'spirit' and is the most nebulous of the five fundamental substances. It is also sometimes translated as 'awareness' and is said to be seen in the alert brightness of the eyes when someone is fully conscious of their surroundings, actions and capabilities. If *shen* is weakened then the eyes are said to lacklustre and thinking can become muddled. Like congenital *jing*, *shen* is something we inherit from our parents, although unlike congenital *jing* it can be nurtured and encouraged throughout our lives by a healthy lifestyle that allows plenty of time for meditation and exercise therapies.

The concept of the shen (spirit) goes back to the early Taoists and incorporates such ideas as god and mind.

Tangible aspects

Although referred to as spirit, *shen* is seen in Chinese theory as having more tangible aspects: it exists as a fundamental substance within the body and is part of the body. In the West, body and spirit have been seen as separate entities since the 17th century but in Chinese philosophy this division has never occurred.

Shen disharmonies can manifest as insomnia, confusion or forgetfulness. More severe forms can include speech problems, with incoherent rambling or even, in extreme cases, psychotic illnesses, violent madness, severe hallucinations or unconsciousness. Just as *jing* is stored in the Kidney, so *shen* is stored in the Heart with Heart disharmonies also damaging the spirit. It is not unusual to find people suffering from Heart weakness or irregularity showing signs of *shen* impairment with disordered speech, conversation that jumps from one topic to another with no clear thread or, in severe cases, the sort of manic behaviour associated with bouts of dementia.

Shen is not confined to medicine but is an important concept in Chinese philosophy and some sources give it as many as 11 different meanings including god, mind, respect, expression, rule, magic and caution. It is sometimes translated as soul – but that simply adds further confusion when considering other terms, such as *hun* (spiritual soul) and *po* (physical soul).

Meditation can be used to channel and cultivate spirit.

SPIRITUAL ASPECTS

The combined spirit of a person – *shen qi* – is said to live in the Heart by day and the Liver by night: during the day its quality can be assessed by the eyes, which in health can be seen as a shining light in the pupils. At night it can be monitored in dreams with a lack of dreams said to indicate a calm and contented Spirit.

FIVE ASPECTS OF SPIRIT

Just as there are five solid organs, five hollow organs and so on, there are five defined aspects of spirit: *hun, po, zhi, yi* and *shen*.

Two contrasting aspects are *hun* and po. *Hun* is a more ethereal aspect of soul and controls conscious and unconscious thoughts. *Po* is sometimes translated as 'animal soul' or 'physical soul', and directs physical energies and vitality; *Hun* resides in the Liver; *po* is stored in the Lung.

Zhi, which resides in the Kidneys, is associated with wants and desires as well as with developing wisdom. *Yi*, stored in the Spleen, controls reflection and intention. *Yi* makes change possible and in Spleen Deficiency sufferers sometimes lack the ability to make these changes.

Finally, *shen* resides in the Heart but is not quite the same as the total *shen qi*, which comprises all five aspects of spirit/soul. In this spiritual context *shen* is associated with propriety and correctness so that disharmonies of the Heart can lead to erratic behaviour.

During the day the shen qi *or spirit is said to be seen in the brightness of the eyes.*

CAUSES OF DISEASE AND DIAGNOSTICS

CAUSES OF DISEASE

When the theories of Chinese medicine were first formulated more than 4,000 years ago, the causes of any disease could be described only in terms of symptoms and effects. There were no machines to identify precisely what was going on in the human body, so the symptoms defined the condition.

In the *Yellow Emperor's Classic of Internal Medicine* only two causes of disease were identified: climatic factors and dysfunction of the human body. Exterior causes were labelled as *yang* while those coming from within the body were described as *yin* diseases. According to the *Nei Jing*, the external disorders could be caused by rain, wind, cold or summer heat, while the internal problems may have their roots in improper diet, irregular life, intemperate sexuality, extreme joy or anger.

Later, in around CE 300, another classic text, entitled the *Synopsis of the Golden Chamber* and written by Zhang Zhongjing, expanded this definition to include three 'injuries'. These could be injuries to the Channels and collateral meridians caused by pathogenic factors invading the internal organs; injury to the body surface by pathogenic factors that then enter the body and eventually obstruct the flow of Blood. Thirdly, there were injuries caused by

factors such as wounds. Today these are described as 'pathogenic' factors (evil *qi*) which may be 'endogenous', 'exogenous' or 'neither endogenous or exogenous'. These pathogenic factors cause disease when they upset the balance between *yin* and *yang* or *qi* and Blood – a balance that is also sometimes called the 'unity of opposites'.

Heat relates to external disorders.

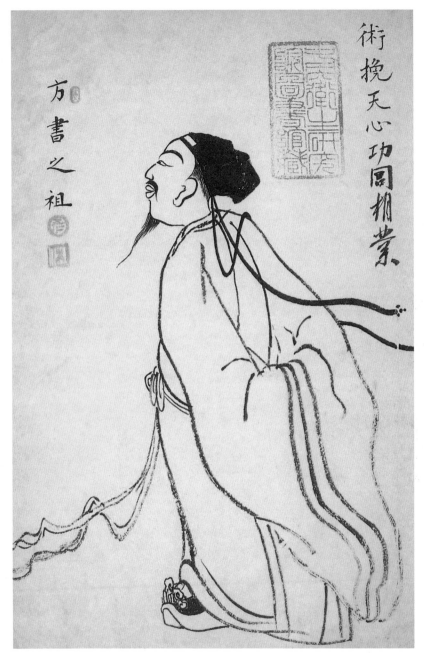

術挽天心功回相業

方書之祖

Zhang Zhongjing is one of China's earliest physicians.

EXTERNAL CAUSES OF DISEASE: THE SIX EVILS

To the Yellow Emperor and his contemporaries, external causes of disease were to do with the climate – seasonal disorders bringing regular and predictable illnesses. This was a view also held by the ancient Greeks and ancient Egyptians and even now we still talk of catching a cold rather than contracting a virus or infection.

The climate in central China was, and is, a matter of extremes: freezing winters, sweltering summers and, at times, persistent winds blowing across the Asian steppes. Small wonder then that the exogenous pathogenic factors, known as the six evils (*liu yin*) were defined as:

• Wind (*feng*)

• Cold (*han*)

• Heat (*re*)

• Dampness (*shi*)

• Dryness (*zao*)

• Fire (*huo*).

Wind, Heat, Fire and Dryness are all regarded as *yang* evils while Cold and Damp are classified as *yin*.

Achieving a balance

While these evils can bring disease they are also essential to life: no wet season and there are no crops, no summer sun and crops will not ripen. However, if the six evils become excessive or abnormally extreme or if the body is weakened then these exogenous pathogens will upset the body's inner balance leading to ill health. Typically, disease is not caused by a single pathogenic factor but by a combination such as Wind-Heat or Cold-Damp. The external pathogens invade the body from the exterior via the skin, mouth or nose and, if not treated at that stage, can go on to affect internal organs.

Occasionally, the six evils can also originate from within the body due to organ dysfunction, but the effects are generally regarded as similar to external attack.

Icy winters were seen as a cause of disease with too much cold leading to ill health.

WIND

Although Wind (*feng*) is associated with spring, pathogenic Wind problems can occur at any time of year. Wind is *yang* in nature, moving outwards and upwards and tends to attack *yang* parts of the body, notably the surface and upper parts including head, upper torso and limbs. Since it attacks the body surface, sweating is often a symptom.

Wind disorders tend to have sudden onset and are characterized by rapid change with variable symptoms.

Wind can also occur in constant movement so diseases that involve abnormal motion – such as dizziness, tremors, convulsions or unusual spasms – are also linked to Wind.

The Liver is susceptible to pathogenic Wind.

ASSOCIATED SYMPTOMS AND DISORDERS

Exogenous Wind is the cause of common colds with fever, sweating, sore throat, cough, catarrh and aversion to wind.

Wind-Cold leads to an intolerance of both wind and cold with fever, headache or more general aches and pains, nasal catarrh and cough. Unlike exogenous Wind in this form of attack there is no sweating.

Wind-Heat symptoms include fever, sweating, headache, reddened eyes, sore throat, sensitivity to light, thirst, cough with thick yellow sputum, breathing problems, constipation and possible nose bleeds.

Wind-Dampness is much like a common cold but with pain in the limbs, lethargy, nausea, loss of appetite and diarrhoea, or as arthritis with pain shifting between various joints and muscles, which is often affected by changes in the weather.

Endogenous Wind attacks the Liver leading to dizziness, muscle spasms, convulsions and sudden coma.

COLD

Cold (*han*) is associated with winter and is characterized by the same phenomena associated with the season: lack of motion, freezing or coagulation. Cold is a *yin* pathogen and inhibits *yang qi* suppressing defensive energies. If it enters the body Cold tends to affect the Spleen and Stomach upsetting the normal distribution of nutrients and water.If Cold attacks the body surface then headaches and generalized aches and pains follow.

Cold causes contraction, closing the pores of the skin and tightening muscles thus affecting the circulation of *yang qi* with muscle spasms that may affect the limbs or abdomen. Cold particularly affects the kidney.

Cold diseases are associated with pain as cold is still and causes stagnation.

ASSOCIATED SYMPTOMS AND DISORDERS

Superficial Exogenous Cold is typified by intolerance to cold, fever without sweating, pains in the neck, aching joints, coughing. There may also be problems with breathing.

Interior Exogenous Cold occurs when Cold injures the Stomach and Spleen or impairs Kidney *yang* – symptoms include aversion to cold, shivering, numbness, high facial colour and purple lips, diarrhoea, flatulence, abdominal pain relieved by heat, poor appetite, vomiting and muscle rigidity.

Wind-Cold-Dampness with predominant Cold is a form of arthritis with Wind-Cold-Damp in the channels and joints that can be relieved by heat and is worse in cold weather.

Endogenous Cold is when both *yang* and *qi* are deficient and symptoms include intolerance of cold, cold hands and feet, vomiting with clear fluid, watery stools, excessive urination. Lethargy and tiredness with some localized pain are not uncommon.

HEAT

Pathogenic Heat (*re*) is closely associated with climate and appears only in hot summers.

It leads to an excess of *yang qi*, and this results in high fever, thirst and sweating. It can also decrease body fluids with excessive sweating and *qi* Deficiency.

Heat disorders often occur with pathogenic Dampness associated with summer's increase in humidity.

ASSOCIATED SYMPTOMS AND DISORDERS

Exposure to Summer Heat is generally a mild condition that includes thirst, dry lips, sweating, possible feverishness, headache, lethargy and nausea.

Heat Stroke is a more severe progression of exposure to Summer Heat with increased nausea, fever, sweating and restlessness; severe cases may involve coma and cold limbs.

Damp-Heat When combined with Damp, Heat gives rise to chills and fever, restlessness, thirst, nausea, poor breathing, poor appetite, lethargy, loose stools and reduced urination.

Excess heat can combine with humidity to cause Damp-Heat syndromes.

DAMPNESS

In Chinese medicine, Dampness (*shi*) is associated with late summer. Pathogenic Damp is also linked to wet, rainy weather and can be a problem for those living or working in damp places. Damp can also originate inside the body, usually from Spleen dysfunction.

Damp is a *yin* factor so can damage the normal flow of *qi* and affect *yang*. Dampness is also perceived as heavy so has a downward motion with swelling in the legs. It also creates sticky secretions, such as mucus in the stools, cloudy urine, vaginal discharge or weeping eczema.

While problems associated with Damp can be difficult to clear. This is because the nature of Damp is stagnant so Damp illnesses tend to spread and recur.

Pathogenic Dampness can be caused both by excess humidity and seasonal rains and wet weather.

ASSOCIATED SYMPTOMS AND DISORDERS

Exogenous Dampness affects the normal flow of *qi* leading to vomiting, nausea and feelings of oppression in the chest and upper abdomen. There can also be poor appetite, reduced urination and constipation. Exogenous Dampness can also cause arthritic pains with heaviness in the joints and difficulties in moving.

Wind-Dampness with predominant Dampness is associated with both the common cold and arthritis, and the condition is more likely to manifest as low fever, lethargy and pain in the limbs.

Endogenous Dampness is generally associated with fluid retention due to Deficient Spleen with symptoms such as poor appetite, nausea, lack of thirst, a feeling of fullness in the abdomen and head, lethargy, diarrhoea, oedema and abnormal vaginal discharge.

DRYNESS

Dryness (*zao*) in Chinese theory is associated with the season of autumn, when leaves start to dry out and eventually turn brown. Pathogenic Dryness is a *yang* factor that depletes body fluids causing dryness in the mouth, nose and throat as well as dry, chapped skin, constipation, and reduced urine.

Typically, Dryness attacks the Lung and Kidney as well as their related *fu* organs, the Large Intestine and Urinary Bladder. Kidney *yin* is important in developing body fluids and is depleted by pathogenic Dryness leading to deficiency. Equally, Kidney or Lung weakness can reduce fluid production and result in Endogenous Dryness.

ASSOCIATED SYMPTOMS AND DISORDERS

Exogenous Dryness (warm) is associated with hot weather with symptoms including fever, dry cough, aversion to cold, headache and restlessness.

Exogenous Dryness (cool) is associated with Dryness and is typified by fever, an aversion to cold, headache, and dry cough as well as an absence of sweating, blocked nose, and dry mouth and throat.

Endogenous Dryness often results in dry mouth and throat, dry, rough skin, dull hair, reduced urine, dry stools and weight loss.

The brown leaves of autumn typify the concept of pathogenic Dryness, which can cause fevers.

FIRE

Fire (*huo*) can occur at any time of the year and is a *yang* pathogen mainly affecting the head since Fire's motion is rapidly upwards. Fire in the Heart, for example, which is linked to the tongue, tends to produce ulcers and soreness in that part of the mouth. Fire in the Liver is associated with sore, red eyes.

Fire problems can also damage body fluids and can lead to 'Fire stirring up Wind', a condition that generally affects the Liver Channel and can lead to coma, high fever and delirium. Fire also increases the flow of Blood, which can damage the blood vessels and lead to various forms of bleeding, from nose bleeds and blood in the urine to internal haemorrhages. Internal or endogenous Fire can be caused by a disharmony between *yin* and *yang*, which can lead either to Excess *yang* or Deficient *yin*.

Fire's motion is upwards, so Fire-related symptoms often affect the head and face.

ASSOCIATED SYMPTOMS AND DISORDERS

Exogenous Fire is associated with infectious diseases and high fever, sweating, thirst, intolerance of heat, preference for cold drinks and, in severe cases, delirium, unconsciousness and bleeding (due to fire stirring up Endogenous Wind).

Endogenous Fire (Excess *yang*) may cause Heart, Liver, Lung and Stomach to be affected with typical symptoms including mouth ulcers, pink eyes, a bitter taste in the mouth, anxiety, dry and sore throat, yellow sputum, painful gums, thirst, constipation and strongly concentrated urine.

Endogenous Fire (Deficient yin) may cause Lung, Kidney, Heart and Liver to be affected with typical symptoms including insomnia and night sweats, a hot sensation on the palms of the hand or soles of the feet, dry throat and eyes, dizziness. There may also be ringing in the ears.

INTERNAL CAUSES OF DISEASE: THE SEVEN EMOTIONS

In traditional Chinese theory, internal disease is believed to be produced by emotional upsets, in turn caused by the seven emotions (*qi qing*). Each of the five *zang* organs (see pages 20–25) is associated with a particular emotion and any imbalance in this emotion – excess or deficiency – can lead to the dysfunction of the relevant organ.

In everyday life emotions are seen as the normal reaction to external events, and it is only when these emotions become extreme or are missing altogether, that they are seen as pathogenic factors.

Although there are only five organs, there are seven defined emotions with two associated with both Heart and Lung:

• Joy (*xi*)

• Anger (*nu*)

• Sadness (*bei*)

• Worry (*si*)

• Fear (*kong*)

• Grief (*you*)

• Shock or Fright (*jing*).

The Heart plays a pivotal role in emotional disorders as it is said to house consciousness and govern all the *zang-fu* organs so emotional stimuli are believed to attack the Heart first before moving on to the relevant organ.

The different emotions are also believed to disrupt the normal flow of *qi*. According to the *Yellow Emperor's Classic of Internal Medicine* (*Nei Jing*) Anger causes *qi* to flow upwards while Fear causes it to descend and Worry leads to *qi* stagnation. Both the Heart and Liver are especially susceptible to emotional disorders.

JOY

Joy (*xi*) is the emotion associated with the Heart; it encourages the circulation of *qi* and Blood and is seen as a beneficial emotion.

Excessive joy is seen as a negative emotion that can damage Heart qi.

However, Excess Joy, in Chinese theory, is seen as over-exuberance verging on mania.

One has to remember that these theories evolved in a hierarchical, ordered society that was very different to our own. In today's world the noisy, excited behaviour of teenagers shouting together in the street, for example, would not be seen as negative aspects of Joy likely to damage the Heart and also possibly affect the Lung. Excess Joy is said to scatter Heart *qi* leading to an inability to concentrate. The sort of hysterical laughter associated with some forms of mental disorder is also associated by the Chinese with damaged Heart *qi*.

ANGER

The emotion associated with the Liver is anger (*nu*) and an excess can affect the flow of Liver *qi*, which interrupts over-all circulation of *qi* and Blood. It can also lead to *qi* stagnation while the ascending Liver *qi* can interfere with normal Lung *qi* action causing certain disharmonies here as well.

Typical symptoms of this disruptive, ascendant Liver *qi* include irritability, headaches, dizziness, flushed face, red eyes and a bitter taste in the mouth. There may also be dryness in the throat or a sensation of something stuck in the throat and pains in the ribs. Symptoms may also include feelings of suffocation and depression.

In women, anger can be related to menstrual irregularities and breast lumps; normalizing Liver *qi* is an important approach in treating various gynaecological problems such as premenstrual syndrome. In extreme cases the disruption of normal Blood and *qi* flow can lead to unconsciousness or choking if Lung *qi* is severely affected.

SADNESS

Sadness (*bei*) is linked to the Lung with excessive melancholy interrupting normal flow of Lung *qi*, causing stagnation with feelings of oppression in the chest and depression.

If Lung *qi* becomes stagnant for a long time it can lead to Fire, which affects the vital essence of the Lung, which in turn can harm the Spleen, thereby disturbing digestive function with loss of appetite, insomnia and weight loss.

WORRY

Worry (*si*) is associated with the Spleen, the prime *zang* organ involved in digestion so any damage to Spleen *qi* can cause problems with distributing nutrients and water to the body. While the emotion linked to the Spleen can be translated as worry, it is also sometimes referred to as pensiveness or over-thinking.

The Chinese say that pensiveness originates from the Heart and occupies one's hearing and makes one's mind concentrate. Prolonged over-thinking can thus also lead to Stagnation of Heart *qi* with symptoms of Heart disease such as strong palpitations, anxiety, weakness in the limbs, disturbed sleep, forgetfulness, and in severe cases, dementia. Some types of menstrual irregularities can also be associated with this type of *qi* Stagnation.

Worry is the emotion associated with the Spleen.

Prolonged Stagnation of Heart and Spleen *qi* leads to a syndrome called 'Depressed Heat in the Heart and Spleen', with symptoms such as loss of appetite, constipation, mouth ulcers, insomnia, palpitations, anxiety and a tendency to be easily startled.

FEAR

Perhaps not surprisingly, Fear (*kong*) is linked to the Kidney; almost all of us have a tendency for increased frequency of urination when we are frightened or nervous.

Fear differs from Shock or Fright, in that Fear is said to originate from timidity within the body and is linked to reduced functionality of the internal organs whereas Shock comes from external sources.

Fear injures the Kidney by causing the normally upward flow of Kidney *qi* to reverse and descend. This leads to low back pains, increased urination, incontinence, lethargy, listlessness, weakness in the legs and feet and a desire for solitude. In women it can cause excessively long menstrual periods and irregular menstruation. Bedwetting in children can also be explained in these terms with severe shyness, insecurity or timidity leading to internally generated Fear, which in turn causes incontinence.

GRIEF

Like Sadness, Grief (*you*) is associated with the Lung. Excessive Grief damages Lung *qi* and since it controls the *qi* flow through the body, can result in more generalized *qi* stagnation with reduced functionality among all the internal organs. Symptoms can include pallor, problems with breathing, a sensation of suffocation in the chest area, general lethargy, depression and loss of appetite, constipation and difficulty with urination, and frequent sighing. Breathing problems and associated conditions such as bronchial asthma are commonly seen in the recently bereaved.

SHOCK OR FRIGHT

Shock (*jing*) is due to external factors rather than internal and is more like a state of panic than an internal nagging fear. It is associated with the Heart and leads to a general dysfunction of *qi*, with the Heart *qi* said to 'wander about, adhering to nothing'. Symptoms include palpitations that may be strong and continual, mental restlessness, cold sweats and a tendency to be easily startled – the sort of symptoms which in the West we might label a 'panic attack'. Unexplained crying or upsets in babies and infants are often attributed to Fright.

Grief can lead to such disorders as bronchial asthma.

OTHER CAUSES OF DISEASE

Chinese traditional medicine also defines a range of other causes of disease that are considered neither external/climatic nor internal/emotional. They include irregular diet, excess sexual activity and physical exertion, excess Phlegm and Blood Stasis.

IRREGULAR DIET

Sometimes defined as an internal cause of disease, irregular diet is seen as an important pathogenic factor. It can injure Spleen and Stomach by disturbing the normal pattern of processing and distributing nutrients and water through the body leading to disruption in the flow of *qi*, Blood and body fluids. With these normal flows disrupted there can be a build-up in Damp leading to the production of Phlegm and symptoms of endogenous Heat. Over time these disruptions can affect other organs causing serious illness. In Chinese theory irregular diet can have three distinct causes: volume, improper food, and rotten or infected food.

Volume of food
Food should be taken in the right quantities and at the right time. Both an excess of food or eating too little can lead to disease. Eating too little food means there are insufficient nutrients to transform into *qi* and Blood, resulting in weakness in vital energy and weakened *wei qi*, causing a likely increase in external illness.

Too much food damages Spleen and Stomach leading to a range of conditions that include abdominal distention, belching, foul-smelling stools and an accumulation of undigested food that is transformed into Heat and may produce Phlegm. Traditionally, meals are eaten at 6 am, 12 noon and 6 pm – believed to be the correct intervals between meals for ideal digestion.

Improper food
This may owe much to an imbalance in what is available locally, such as the traditional shortage of fruits in winter, or it could be associated with personal preferences and the avoidance of certain food groups. Either factor can lead to disorders such as goitre, rickets, night blindness and beriberi.

Foods need to avoid being too 'hot' or too 'cold' to prevent disharmony – 'cold' prawns with 'hot' chillies create the perfect balance, for example.

Personal preferences are particulalry significant. Too much raw or cold food, for example, is said to lead to Spleen and Stomach Deficiency, with abdominal pains and diarrhoea. Too much spicy or pungent food, in contrast, impairs the vital essence of the Stomach, leading to a condition called 'Excess Stomach Heat', with feelings of hunger, indigestion, vertigo and possibly ulcers and boils.A diet that involves too much alcohol is believed to cause an increase in Damp, Heat and Phlegm, with ancient texts describing the resulting abdominal masses and related weight loss in much the same terms that a modern physician would define cirrhosis.

Rotten or infected food

Eating bad food causes what most people would call food poisoning, with nausea, vomiting, diarrhoea, abdominal pain or dysentery.

EXCESS SEXUAL ACTIVITY AND PHYSICAL EXERTION

Sometimes classified as another internal cause of disease, too much sexual activity is believed to consume *jing* and damage Kidney *qi* leading to Deficiency with lower back pains, aching knee joints, dizziness, tinnitus, and lethargy. In men there may also be impotence and nocturnal emissions while women typically suffer from menstrual irregularities and vaginal discharge.

In contrast, too much physical exertion weakens primordial *qi* leading to reduced functionality in all the *zang-fu* organs, with general sluggishness, lethargy, apathy and breathing disorders. Like excess Worry or over-thinking, excess physical activity can also affect Heart *qi* with resulting palpitations, insomnia, forgetfulness and disturbed sleep.

Too little physical exertion can be just as damaging, with a deficiency in vital energy and reduced *wei qi* since circulation of both *qi* and Blood will be slow. Symptoms include poor appetite, lethargy, weakness in the limbs, vertigo and palpitations.

EXCESS PHLEGM

Phlegm in Chinese medicine is quite different from the 'phlegm' that Western medicine associates with catarrhal conditions and sputum. Phlegm, in this context, is believed to develop from Water and Fluid retained in the body. Phlegm can be visible or invisible: the visible appears as sputum but the invisible collects inside the body and can be the cause of disease and its result.

In Chinese theory the Spleen separates the clear and turbid fluids produced during digestion. If these turbid fluids are not excreted but retained because of some failure in

In Chinese medicine an excess of energetic exercise is seen as harmful.

the water transport system, then they can develop into Phlegm. This failure can be due to *qi* weakness in Lung, Spleen or Kidney or may be associated with obstructions in the Triple Burner (*san jiao*) disrupting the normal Fluid transport mechanisms.

Pathogenic (invisible) Phlegm can collect anywhere in the body, in any of the *zang-fu* organs or in superficial tissues such as tendons and skin. There may be visible external signs of Phlegm, such as oedema, oozing fluid from inflammations or palpable lymph nodes. Internal symptoms can include mental disturbances, blockages in the Channels or accumulations of Phlegm in specific organs. If Phlegm builds up in the Heart, for example, there will be mental disturbances, such as schizophrenia or mania while Phlegm in the Lungs can cause asthmatic symptoms or productive coughs with characteristics wheezy breathing described as 'the sound of Phlegm'.

Stagnation in the Stomach can cause nausea and vomiting, while in the Channels it can lead to sensations of numbness and partial paralysis.

BLOOD STASIS

Blood Stagnation or Stasis is another of the possible internal causes of disease. Blood, in Chinese medicine, is not the same as the usual Western anatomical concept of blood and

Blood Stagnation does not imply a thrombosis or massive clot somewhere in the circulatory system.

Instead, Stagnant Blood is a pathological product caused when organs fail to work properly; Stasis occurs when Blood flows erratically because of *qi* Deficiency or because of attack by pathogenic Cold. Internal bleeding caused either by trauma or pathogenic Heat can also lead to Blood Stasis.

Stagnant Blood can also cause an obstruction and further interrupt the flow of *qi* and Blood. Once Stasis has developed, the Blood involved is no longer free to circulate in the body moistening the tissues and nourishing the body, and this inevitably leads to additional problems.

Typical symptoms of Blood Stasis vary depending on whereabouts in the body the Blood is stagnating. Generally, however, the symptoms include some sort of pain and swelling. Stagnation in the Lungs, for example, causes chest pain and will lead to the coughing up of blood; in the Liver Stagnation can lead to pain and abdominal masses; in the Stomach to obvious bright-red blood in the stools.

Stagnant Blood in the uterus is the cause of many menstrual problems, including period pain, irregular menstruation and, in some cases, absence of periods.

THE DEVELOPMENT OF DISEASE

While Chinese theory has clearly defined causes of disease, the progression and outcome are not as certain since much depends on the strength of the body to fight back and overcome the illness. It is a contest between the pathogen and what some call anti-pathogenic *qi*.

ANTI-PATHOGENIC QI

Fighting illness, in Chinese theory, is all about balance: it is about adjusting the interaction between *yin* and *yang*, between *qi* and Blood and between the various functions of the *zang-fu* organs in order to defeat the invading pathogen. It is also about prevention: as Zhang Zhongjing in the *Synopsis of the Golden Chamber* put it: 'Keep strong and disease will find no way to attack'.

Four main factors are believed to determine the strength of each individual's anti-pathogenic *qi*:

Constitution This is largely dictated by the attributes inherited from our parents, as well as the primary influences of lifestyle and environment that follow.

Diet This is important among the 'after heaven' influences with both obesity and low body weight affecting how we combat disease.

Mental state In traditional Chinese medicine, a person's mental state has a significant influence on the function of *qi* and Blood. Depression, for example, can lead to poor appetite, organ dysfunction and weakened *wei qi* making the sufferer more susceptible to pathogenic attack.

Poor habits These generally involve excess: excessive sleeping, for example, weakens *qi*; too much sitting harms muscles; too much standing harms bones; or too much walking harms tendons; and excessive concentration on mental work for long hours injures both Heart and Spleen.

Recovery from illness means that anti-pathogenic *qi* has won the battle; deterioration in the condition obviously means the reverse. In Chinese theory most illnesses start from exterior symptoms that move to the interior if the condition worsens. The second stage is the development of Cold symptoms as defeat of anti-

Excessive sleep in Chinese theory is believed to weaken qi.

Chinese physicians monitor signs and symptoms closely to assess the disease progression.

CAUSES OF DISEASE AND DIAGNOSTICS

pathogenic *qi* damages the body's Heat. Finally, Deficiency symptoms develop as anti-pathogenic *qi* weakens even further with, ultimately, life ending when '*yin* and *yang* part and *qi* and Blood run out'. Good treatment is always focused on preventing the illness moving through these consecutive states.

RESTORING BALANCE

Recovery from illness means that the anti-pathogenic *qi* has successfully re-balanced *yin* and *yang*, *qi* and Blood, as well as normalizing the various functions of the *zang-fu* organs. Medical treatment is aimed at identifying the various imbalances and supporting the action of the anti-pathogenic *qi* at each stage.

Vital energy (*yang qi*) and vital essence (*yin* essence) are constantly changing, with vital energy producing Heat and motion upwards while vital essence is associated with Cold and tranquility moving downwards. Imbalance occurs when there is failure of either vital energy or vital essence.

Similarly, *qi* and Blood are mutually interdependent upon one another with Blood being the material basis for generating *qi* and the flow of Blood depending on *qi*. Any weakness in *qi* can lead to a reduction in that flow and thus stagnation of Blood, while a weakness in Blood interrupts the generation of *qi*.

Each of the *zang-fu* organs is either involved in some form of ascending or descending motion. In illness these natural movements can be disrupted causing a range of symptoms that the Chinese physician will use to identify the precise organ weaknesses involved.

There are five ways in which *yang* and *yin* can be disrupted, four interruptions for normal *qi* and Blood function and a great many symptoms that result from interrupting the normal ascending and descending functions of the *zang-fu* organs. Each of these is listed in the tables on the following pages (see pages 70–71).

Failure of ascending and descending motions

Numerous conditions can follow from a failure of the normal motions associated with the *zang-fu* organs. If Lung *qi* fails to descend, for example, there can be coughing and asthmatic problems, while over-exuberant Liver *qi* has an upward motion causing dizziness and headaches. If the downward motion associated with the Large Intestine fails, constipation is likely, while weakness in the Spleen can cause *qi* to descend and so fail to support surrounding tissues. The resulting risk is one of rectal or uterine prolapse.

YIN AND YANG DISRUPTION

	Yang Disruption	Yin Disruption
Dominant	Dominant *yang* is usually caused by pathogenic Heat attacking the body or by pathogenic Cold entering the body and being transformed into Heat.	Dominant *yin* is usually caused by Cold and Damp attacking the exterior and a failure of the *yang qi* to produce warmth.
Deficient	Deficient *yang* is usually from innate insufficiency or after a long illness.	Deficient *yin* is generally due to excessive consumption of vital essence, possibly related to fever.
Perished	Perished *yang* is a serious condition where *yang* becomes detached from the body either because of severe deficiency or extreme Cold.	Perished *yin* is usually due to excess Heat scorching body fluids but also caused by massive haemorrhage, severe diarrhoea or vomiting and generally signifying a critical condition.
Excessive	Excessive *yang* hindering *yin* occurs when dominant *yang* produces excess Heat in the interior that becomes disconnected with *yin* on the exterior.	Excessive *yin* hindering *yang* occurs when too much *yin* creates excess Cold that is trapped within the body and *yang* becomes separated on the exterior.
Impaired	Impaired *yang* impeding the creation of *yin* occurs when persistent deficiency of *yang* reduces the vital essence.	Impaired *yin* impeding the creation of *yang* is caused by over-consumption of vital essence damaging the production of vital energy with, ultimately, a deficiency of both.

INTERRUPTED QI AND BLOOD

Interrupted Qi	Interrupted Blood
Deficient *yang* is usually caused by pathogenic Heat attacking the body or by pathogenic Cold entering the body and being transformed into Heat.	Deficient Blood may be due to massive haemorrhage, a failure of the Spleen and Stomach to transform food and water correctly, or internal damage due to chronic illness or parasites.
Stagnant *yang* is usually from innate insufficiency or after a long illness.	Stagnant Blood is usually where the circulation is damaged by pathogenic factors, traumatic injury or weakened *qi*. In women it can be caused by retention of the lochia after childbirth.
Qi sinking to the middle *jiao yang* is a serious condition where *yang* becomes detached from the body either because of severe deficiency or extreme Cold.	Blood attacked by Heat is when both exogenous and endogenous Heat can damage Blood or external Cold can invade the interior and be transformed into Heat. Emotional depression can also cause Heat by depressing Liver *qi* leading to internal Fire.
Adverse Flow *yang* hindering *yin* occurs when dominant *yang* produces excess Heat in the interior that becomes disconnected with *yin* on the exterior.	Haemorrhage is believed to be caused by an adverse flow of *qi*, external injury or excess Fire.

CHINESE EXAMINATION

Dating back to an age when doctors depended on what they could see, feel and hear rather than a battery of clinical tests, traditional Chinese examination follows an established pattern based on observation and listening. There are four distinct phases to a traditional Chinese examination: inspection; auscultation and olfaction; interrogation; and palpation.

INSPECTION

Inspection is the most important component of the examination and involves studying the patient's appearance, tongue, nose, skin colour and so on. A physician will start the examination from the moment they see the patient: how do they walk or stand? What does that imply about their Spirit – is it alert and lively or dull and downcast? If the body is firm and muscular then *qi* and *jing* are likely to be strong and the person healthy; obesity can suggest Spleen *qi* Deficiency with failure to transform nutrients or possibly a Phlegm or Damp problem. The extremely thin could be suffering from digestive weakness, perhaps middle *jiao* problems or maybe *yin* Deficiency.

The over-active and restless might be suffering from a *yang* syndrome, Excess or Heat while the more passive could have a *yin* imbalance, Deficiency or Cold. Tremors are also significant: in the elderly, trembling hands imply *yin* deficiency, while in younger people this is more likely to be related to a Wind problem.

The colours and shapes seen in the eyes, face, and tongue also each have their own specific significance.

Inspecting the eyes

The eyes are said to be the 'door of the Spirit' and a physician will look for signs of swelling or discoloration. If the Spirit is strong and alert then the eyes are bright; if not they can look dull and blank or glassy – both of which suggest weakened spirit.

Different parts of the eye correspond to different organs so a yellow discharge in the corner of the eye may suggest some sort of problem with Heat in the Heart while swollen eyelids can imply Spleen weakness. Colour is important, too: red eyes suggest some form of Heat problem

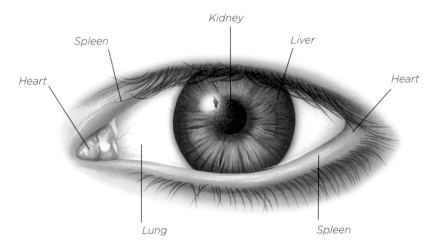

Kidney

Spleen

Liver

Heart

Heart

Lung

Spleen

The Eye

while if the whites of the eyes (the sclera) have a yellowish tinge it suggests Damp.

Inspecting the face

The colour of the face is also of great significance in diagnosis: if the face is very red or flushed, there may be excess Heat or if the flushing only appears in the evening *yin* Deficiency is likely. If it is white or very pale then the opposite is true with a likely Cold syndrome or possible *yang* or *qi* Deficiency. Yellow suggests Damp or Spleen problems while greenish tinges imply either a Cold syndrome or Blood Stagnation.

The location of any unusual colours, inflammations or sores around the nose and cheeks is also indicative of underlying disorders in the *zang-fu* organs. Redness between nose and lip, for example, suggests a uterine problem in women while the areas beneath the eyes are associated with the Kidney.

Different parts of the body are also related through the five-element model to the *zang-fu* organs so the quality of the head hair can provide insights about the Kidney, while abnormally pale lips may suggest a Spleen weakness and broken weak nails some form of Liver dysfunction.

Inspecting the tongue

The tongue is another important pointer in diagnosis with different parts of the tongue relating to different organs of the body, while the colour and type of coating can indicate which pathogenic factors are involved in the illness.

A red tip, for example, could suggest Heat in the Heart while redness to the back of the tongue could imply a Kidney problem. In general a thin, pale tongue implies Deficiency of *qi* and Blood, while cracks in the tongue's surface could suggest a Blood Deficiency and apparent tooth-marks round the edges may imply a problem with Spleen *yang*.

Yellow coatings on the tongue suggest Heat, Damp or endogenous pathogens, while white coatings indicate an exogenous or Cold problem. There are dozens of possible combinations of tongue colour, coating, shape, blemishes and motion and each will suggest a specific syndrome or health problem to the experienced practitioner.

A patient offers his tongue for inspection.

SOME OF THE POSSIBLE HEALTH PROBLEMS ASSOCIATED WITH PARTICULAR TONGUE CONDITIONS

Condition	Possible Problem
Pale	Cold syndrome, *yang* deficiency, *qi* deficiency, Blood deficiency
Reddish	Interior heat syndrome, excess *qi* and Blood, *yin* deficiency
Dark red	Severe endogenous Heat
Purple or blue	Inadequate body fluids, extreme pathogenic Heat
Purplish spots	Blood Stagnation
Black	Internal cold syndrome
Yellow coating	Heat syndrome, Excess Damp or endogenous pathogens
White coating	Cold syndrome or exogenous pathogens
Cracked surface	Consumption of vital essence

AUSCULTATION AND OLFACTION

After inspection comes the listening and smelling: what sort of voice does the patient have? Is their breathing fast or slow, regular or irregular? Are there any abnormal body smells? A loud voice suggests *yang*, Heat and Excess while a soft voice implies *yin*, Cold or Deficiency syndromes. Speech is linked to the Heart so impediments such as stammering or confused words could indicate an underlying Heart disorder.

Chinese practitioners measure breathing rates in comparison to their own rather than resorting to timers and stopwatches. Coughs and hiccups are also analysed; coughing with a low weak voice, for example, suggests Deficiency while loud hiccoughs imply Excess Heat. Strong body odour also suggests a general Heat problem.

A Chinese doctor takes the pulse of a patient during a routine examination.

INTERROGATION

In Chinese theory, the interrogation phase should cover 'The Ten Questions', a routine developed over centuries that is covered during the course of the consultation and, given the specific interpretations of the patient's reply which the Chinese doctor makes, can actually appear quite brief. These questions cover:

- the nature of any chills and fevers

- patterns of perspiration

- the location and type of any pains in the head, body and limbs

- unusual sensations in chest and abdomen

- bowel movements and urination

- appetite

- thirst

- hearing

- previous diseases suffered by the patient and other family members

- onset and development of the present illness.

Women will also be asked about their menstrual cycle or vaginal discharges while the focus in children is likely to be on infectious diseases, any frights, or recent changes in eating patterns.

The aim of The Ten Questions is to understand how the patient's chief complaint fits in with more general information about his or her lifestyle and familial tendencies. It is a routine well understood by Chinese patients who will describe their pain, for example, as distending, stabbing, gaseous, burning, heavy, gnawing, dull, hot or 'accompanied by cold' with very little prompting.

PALPATION

The final stage of the consultation is palpation or touching. As in the West this can include abdominal palpation looking for any lumps or masses as well as feeling the limbs to assess temperature or swellings.

The key difference in Chinese medicine, however, is in the importance placed on taking the pulse or pulses. While a Western practitioner will simply feel the wrist to measure heart rate and check for irregular rhythms, the Chinese doctor will be subtly applying three fingers to each wrist.

The area where the radial artery can be felt on the wrist is known in Chinese as the *cun kou*, with the three finger-width points assessed known as *cun*, *guan* and *chi*.

The *cun* position corresponds to the *taiyuan* point on the Lung meridian and, since all the *zang-fu* organs

and Channels are said to meet in the Lung, it is believed to be the ideal place for measuring their strength.

Pulse positions

While each position equates to one or other of the *zang-fu* organs, there are also different types of pressure applied by the doctor – gentle, firm or hard. These allow the doctor to assess how deeply the illness has penetrated from superficial to deep within the interior. In total, therefore the doctor has nine pulse positions. Each reading takes at least a minute to assess fully.

Classic Chinese texts talk of 28 different types of pulse although modern practitioners tend to focus on 17.

Checking the pulse

A normal healthy pulse is usually described as strong without being 'solid', with regular rhythm and a firm root, and is felt by pressing deeply at the chi position. A Chinese doctor measures pulse by matching it with his or her own steady breathing with the normal rate said to be four or five beats per breath (at a rate of about 18 breaths per minute). What is deemed normal varies between men and women and at different times of year. The female pulse is generally softer, weaker and more rapid than a male pulse, while for both men and women the pulse may appear slightly taut in spring, more full in summer, floating in the autumn and sinking in winter as our *yin-yang* balance changes with the seasons

PULSE POSITIONS

	Left wrist	Right wrist
Cun	Heart/pericardium	Lung
Guan	Liver/Gall Bladder	Spleen/Stomach
Chi	Kidney/Urinary Bladder	Kidney/Small and Large Intestines

TYPES OF PULSE

Opposite patterns of pulse cannot occur together – a pulse cannot be rapid and slow at the same time, for example. However, other characteristics do commonly occur together. A floating, tight pulse could imply a superficial Cold problem while a deep, rapid pulse implies interior Heat, and so on.

Floating pulse is superficial and feels weaker as more pressure is applied, and indicates an Exterior syndrome.

Deep pulse feels stronger when more pressure is applied, and indicates an Interior syndrome – a deep forceful pulse suggests an Excess condition; a weak deep pulse a Deficiency syndrome.

Slow pulse with three or fewer than three beats per breath (less than 60 a minute) suggests Cold or *yang* Deficiency.

Rapid pulse with more than five beats per breath (more than 90 per minute) suggests a Heat condition.

Empty pulse describes the strength of the throb with an empty pulse presenting little force to the pressing fingers. It indicates Deficiency.

Full pulse is where the throbs are clearly perceptible even with little pressure. It suggests Excess.

Slippery pulse is said to feel smooth and flowing. It suggests Excess Heat or Phlegm.

Taut pulse feels like pressing a violin string. It usually suggests Liver or Gall Bladder problems or Phlegm.

Choppy pulse is the opposite of slippery – fine, short and slow, it suggests Stagnant *qi* or Blood, or Blood Deficiency and is common in anaemia.

Overflowing pulse feels like dashing waves that rise forcefully but suddenly decline. It suggests Excess Heat or the advanced stage of an infectious illness.

Thready pulse is a fine pulse that remains clear under heavy pressure. It can indicate Deficiency of *qi* and Blood or of both *yin* and *yang*.

Soft pulse lacks tension and is superficial, soft and fine. It suggests Dampness or Deficiency or may occur in debility when *qi* and Blood are weak.

Tight pulse feels like a tightly stretched cord but is smaller and not so tense as a taut pulse. It can suggest Cold or pain.

Relaxed pulse is loose and appears slow even though it may be at the usual four beats per breath. It suggests pathogenic Damp.

Hasty pulse is rapid with irregular missing beats. It indicates Excess *yang* and Heat with stagnation of Blood and *qi*.

Slow, uneven pulse is slow with irregular missing beats. It indicates blockage of *qi* due to Excess *yin*, Cold, Phlegm or Stagnant Blood.

Intermittent pulse has a normal frequency but a pattern of regular missing beats. This suggests general decline in the *zang* organs such as in severe Heat syndrome, severe pain, fever or fright.

CHINESE DIAGNOSTICS

Disease labels in Western medicine are often either descriptive of the underlying pathological problem causing the illness or of the most significant symptom: arthritis simply means inflammation of the joints; gastritis is inflammation of the stomach, and so on. It is the same with Chinese medicine, only the labels sound very different to Western ears: Deficiency of Heart *qi*, Flaring of Liver Fire, or Blood Stagnation, for example.

Having completed their examination, Chinese physicians apply the Eight Guiding Principles in order to produce a diagnosis.

IDENTIFYING THE DISORDER

Identifying the correct Chinese syndrome is a far more formalized process than with Western differential diagnosis and is based on what are termed the 'Eight Guiding Principles' (*ba gang*). This involves identifying whether the problem is related to Interior or Exterior, Cold or Heat, Deficiency or Excess, *yin* or *yang*. All signs and symptoms of disease, which the doctor has identified from the examination, are classified in these eight categories with a series of additional diagnostic approaches used to refine this basic differentiation and pinpoint the precise syndrome involved.

Traditionally, signs and symptoms in Chinese medicine are seen less as demonstrations of some underlying pathological condition and more as indications of how the body is fighting the invading pathogen. The same 'disease' in Western terms could actually be defined as various different syndromes in Chinese medicine, reflecting how the disease is progressing in the individual patient and how the patient's body is responding depending on the individual strengths and weaknesses.

Eight guiding principles
First the doctor must decide whether the problem is Exterior or Interior: Exterior syndromes tend to be superficial, less severe and short-lived while Interior syndromes are more serious and often chronic. Exterior problems are usually the result of attack by one or other of the external pathogens while Interior syndromes can be associated with:

- more advanced stages of these external diseases
- direct attack on the internal *zang-fu* organs by an exogenous pathogen – by eating too much cold food, for example
- emotional disturbance related to one or other of the seven emotions.

The next stage is to identify whether it is a Cold or a Heat problem. Cold

Each problem is classed as yin *or* yang.

syndromes may be associated with attack by pathogenic Cold or by a dominant *yin* condition associated with *yang* Deficiency, for example. Heat problems might similarly be associated with pathogenic Heat or perhaps by Fire caused by Stagnant *qi* in one of the *zang* organs.

Next comes Excess or Deficiency: Deficiency problems might be associated with weakened defence energy and thus easy success for any invading pathogens, while in Excess problems the anti-pathogenic *qi* is still strong so the struggle between the two produces symptoms of hyperactivity. Deficiency syndromes

tend to be associated with chronic illness and may involve Deficient *yin*, *yang*, *qi* or Blood. Excess syndromes tend to be associated with invading pathogens or some sort of organ problem leading to excess Phlegm, Dampness or Blood Stagnation.

Finally the doctor identifies whether the problem is *yin* or *yang*: Interior, Cold and Deficiency syndromes are *yin* while Exterior, Heat and Excess ones are *yang*. Typically, *yin* syndromes involve weakened *yang*, pathogenic Cold, reduced energy metabolism and insufficient Heat; disorders of Blood or the *zang* organs are also *yin*. Yang syndromes involve dominant internal Heat, *yang qi*, or increased energy metabolism; disorders involving *qi* of the *fu* organs are also *yang*.

REFINING THE DIAGNOSIS

Having applied the Eight Guiding Principles, the Chinese doctor can then further clarify the diagnosis depending on the initial identification.

For internal diseases, for example, the state of both *qi* and Blood need to be considered as there could be Deficiency or Stagnation, adverse flow of *qi*, or 'toxic Heat' in the Blood.

Next any problems with the *zang-fu* organs involved need to be accurately identified; again these are classified as Excess or Deficiency

Cold syndromes involve cold limbs, aching joints, with watery catarrh or diarrhoea.

Chinese doctors may assess how efficiently a patient's body fights invading pathogens.

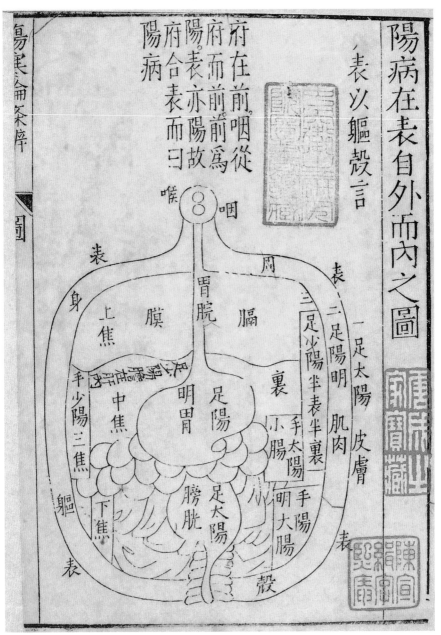

The traditional Chinese view of digestion is very different to that of modern understanding, involving the Spleen and san jiao.

problems. Some heart diseases or anaemia cases, for example, would be classified as due to Deficiency of Heart *yin* or Heart Blood, while chronic bronchitis might be associated with an Excess syndrome that is caused by Wind-Cold invading the Lung.

Theory of six Channels

The doctor may also apply the Theory of the six Channels: problems associated with *taiyin*, *shaoyin*, and *jueyin* are described as syndromes of the *yin* Channels, while those involving *yangming*, *taiyang*, and *shaoyang* are *yang*. The Channels are associated with either Interior, Exterior or both Interior and Exterior disorders, so by considering a patient's symptoms the doctor can identify the affected Channel, which then helps pinpoint the organs affected as well as whether the problem is Interior or Exterior. It also helps to predict the likely progression of the illness as the Channels are linked so the doctor can understand which organ may next be affected as the illness progresses.

Theory of wei, qi, ying and xue

Other diagnostic techniques focus on specific groups of diseases. The 'Theory of *wei*, *qi*, *ying* and *xue*', for example, was developed by Ye Tianshi (1667–1746) in his book *Wen Re Lun* (*On Febrile Disease*), and helps to identify syndromes associated with pathogenic Heat. A *wei* syndrome involves a superficial attack on the body's surface, *qi* further involves the body's defence mechanisms, *ying* is an attack on the body's system of processing and distributing nutrients, while *xue* is Heat attacking the Blood. These four stages define the progression of attack by pathogenic Heat (infectious disease).

Theory of the Triple Burner

Differentiating Damp-Heat syndromes in infectious diseases uses the 'Theory of the Triple Burner' developed by Wu Jutong (1758–1836) in the *Wen Bing Tiao Bian* (Treatise on Differentiation and Treatment of Seasonal Warm Diseases) completed in 1798. This argues that epidemic diseases are either Warm-Heat or Damp-Heat. Damp-Heat diseases, largely confined to the *wei* and *qi* stages, which penetrate the *san jiao* (Triple Burner). From the patient's symptoms it is possible to identify which part of the *san jiao* – lower, middle or upper – is affected and so deliver the appropriate treatment.

With both these theories it is worth remembering that doctors of the 17th and 18th centuries were much preoccupied with epidemic and infectious disorders, such as plague, smallpox, typhoid or cholera that could often be fatal. Today, these 'febrile diseases' are more likely to be treated with antibiotics.

IDENTIFYING DISHARMONIES

The aim of the various diagnostic techniques is to use the Eight Guiding Principles in order to identify how the *zang-fu* organs are affected by external or internal pathogens and thus what the appropriate treatment may be.

Headaches may have a variety of causes in Chinese medicine.

External disorders

External diseases are superficial and most commonly involve Wind, Damp and Cold affecting the Lung, producing symptoms that Westerners describe as a common cold but in Chinese terms would be classified as Wind and/or Cold and/or Damp invading the Lung. A severe common cold may see Wind, Cold or Damp moving into the Lungs causing symptoms that Westerners might call 'flu-like'.

The other *zang* organs are more likely to be affected by internal causes such as the seven emotions, or by a failure to treat external pathogens in the early stages.

Internal disorders

Internal disorders commonly involve Heat, Damp, and Cold with Wind, which may be blamed for causing blockages in the Channels leading to pain. Too much Heat in the Heart, for example, can upset Blood circulation and mental activities since these are controlled by the Heart. Emotional disorders can be caused as well since the Heart stores Spirit, so disharmony can lead to insomnia and confusion.

Specific problems

Too much Heat in the Liver can lead to a Flaring of Liver Fire with excessive anger and irritability; it could damage Liver *yin* or interfere with the regular flow of *qi* since this is another Liver function. The Blood can also be affected, since the Liver stores Blood.

Too much Damp in the Spleen can interfere with its ability to transport and transform fluids leading to digestive disorders and problems with urinary functions. Spleen Deficiency can cause a build-up of Phlegm that can cause problems elsewhere in the system.

The Kidney can typically be affected by an excess of Cold and Damp, which can lead to Kidney *yang* Deficiency, while too much Heat can damage Kidney *yin*. If Kidney *qi* is weakened then Lung disorders such as asthma can follow since the Kidney helps the Lung to manage respiration. Kidney Deficiency also upsets water regulation leading to diarrhoea or pain in the bones.

Diagnosis and treatment

In theory, the imbalances listed above, and others, will be identified by the Chinese physician during an examination, and appropriate treatment – including herbal brews, acupuncture, exercise routines or dietary advice – can then be given. Treatment is designed to strengthen the body and restore balance. Regular monitoring is required throughout treatment to see how the patient reacts to the each new stage of the disorder as his or her recovery progresses.

CHINESE SYNDROMES

While it is fairly easy for non-experts to understand such concepts as *qi* Deficiency, there are many syndrome names that seem confusing and incomprehensible. They date back to a time when fatal epidemic diseases were far more prevalent than they are today. Illnesses that are now successfully treated with modern drugs, or have been virtually eradicated thanks to vaccination programmes, were of largely unknown cause and often fatal in earlier centuries.

Many of the names developed as descriptions of illnesses and still appear in Chinese herbals or may be found on websites selling Chinese patent remedies. Some of the syndromes that are commonly mentioned include:

Abandoned Syndrome (*tuo zheng*) is typified by heavy sweating, sagging jaw, closed eyes, incontinence and a small thin pulse. This is due to severe injury to *qi*, Blood, *yin* and *yang* so that the patient is 'abandoned' by their essential *qi*. The condition is likely to be caused by a stroke (cerebrovascular accident).

'Cock-crow diarrhoea' (*wu geng xie*) has symptoms of abdominal pain and wind early in the morning, which is relieved by evacuation of the bowels and is associated with Deficient Kidney *yang*.

Fire Poison (*huo du*) is any disorder with severe Heat and Poison where the patient feels sick; usually caused by boils, abscesses, carbuncles or soft tissue inflammations.

Indeterminate Gnawing Hunger (*cao za*) is an unpleasant sensation of apparent pain and hunger when there is neither and is associated with peptic ulcers and gastritis.

Painful Obstruction (*bi*) are disorders associated with blockages in the Channels (meridians) usually associated with external pathogens. Bì syndrome is most commonly associated with arthritis but may also affect any of the *zang-fu* organs.

Restless Organ Syndrome (*zang zao*) is typified by inappropriate behaviour, insomnia, mania and restlessness that may be due to frustration caused by Constrained Liver *qi* or excessive worrying caused by Deficient Spleen. In the West it would have been described as 'hysteria'.

Steaming Bone Syndrome

(*gu zheng*) is a deficient *yin* fever characterized by a sensation of heat radiating from the bones to the skin, with night sweats, breathing problems and disturbed sleep; often associated with pulmonary tuberculosis.

Wasting and Thirsting Syndrome

(*xiao ke bing*) is typified by extreme and constant thirst, emaciation and excessive urination and now equated with diabetes.

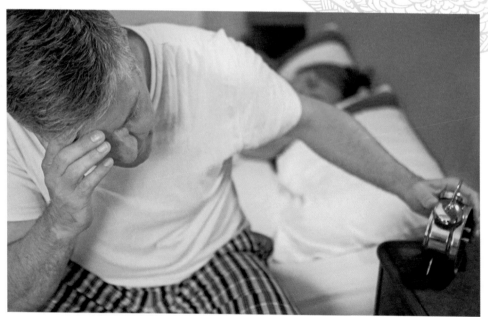

Insomnia is associated with Restless Organ Syndrome.

APPLYING CHINESE DIAGNOSIS

Common ailments defined in Western terms can take on a whole new meaning when Chinese medicine diagnostics are applied.

In Chinese theory, common colds have many different causes.

COMMON COLD

Common colds – involving one or more of the following, catarrh, sneezing, headache, chills, cough or sore throat, are usually treated in the West with an assortment of products providing symptomatic relief – Aspirin, cough mixtures, nasal sprays, chest rubs and so on.

In Chinese theory such colds are generally regarded as being caused by external pathogens and become more severe or flu-like if the external pathogens are strong enough to invade the Channels.

The nature of the pathogen determines the symptoms the sufferer will endure and these will guide the doctor in prescribing the correct remedy to support the body's anti-pathogenic qi.

Symptoms

The cold's onset is often linked to abnormal weather so the doctor will always take note of the prevailing climatic conditions at the time the cold began. Obviously, modern Chinese medicine practitioners accept that contagious infections can also cause colds – not just external 'evils' – but treatment is still based on an analysis of symptoms and the body's reaction to the pathogen rather than taking a single one-size-fits-all approach.

Treatments

Colds due to pathogenic Wind-Cold, for example, generally involve chills, watery catarrh, an absence of sweating, sneezing, headaches, aching joints, ticklish throat, cough with little sputum, a pale coating to the tongue and a floating or tight pulse. Such colds are treated with warming, pungent herbs such as gui zhi (cinnamon twigs) or zi su zi (perilla seeds).

A cold due to Wind-Heat would be typified by a high fever, sweating, headache, thick nasal catarrh, a dry and sore throat, cough with sticky sputum, a yellow tongue coating with the tongue red at the edges and tip, and a floating, rapid pulse. Appropriate herbs this time are pungent and cool such as bo he (field mint), niu bang zi (burdock seeds) or ju hua (chrysanthemum flowers).

Seasonal colds have their distinct symptoms and remedies. A cold due to pathogenic Dryness in autumn, for example, is characterized by fever, chills, headache, a dry unproductive cough, thirst, dry mouth and nose, minimal saliva, red tongue with thin coating and a floating and rapid pulse. Remedies may include herbs that are more moistening to clear the Dryness as well as soothe the Lung and increase saliva, such as sang ye (mulberry leaf) or jie geng (balloon flower root).

PREMENSTRUAL SYNDROME

For many women premenstrual syndrome (PMS) is a monthly nightmare with symptoms that can include bouts of anger, irritability and depression, abdominal bloating, diarrhoea and/or constipation, food cravings, breast swelling or tenderness, headaches and insomnia. In Western medicine premenstrual symptoms are often blamed on hormonal imbalance.

In Chinese theory the Liver stores Blood and is thus closely associated with menstruation. It also regulates the flow of *qi* so any problems with the Liver are likely to impede *qi* flow leading to Obstructions and Stagnation elsewhere in the body.

During the examination a Chinese doctor will ask questions about the menstrual blood – if dark and clotted, for example, this could indicate Stagnation of *qi* and Blood: *qi* moves Blood so if *qi* Stagnates so does Blood. Such Stagnation in the lower abdomen can be caused by some sort of damage to Liver *qi*. Breast swelling can also be traced back to Liver problems with branch collaterals of the foot *jueyin* meridian (the Liver Channel) supplying the nipple while the Stomach meridian also crosses the breasts.

The Liver is also associated with the emotion anger and the sound of shouting. PMS is often followed by a painful period – another indication of Stagnating *qi* and Blood.

A sign of congestion

Rather than being hormonal, Chinese medicine regards PMS as a sign of Congested Liver *qi*. From the five-phase model the Chinese doctor will also know that an overforceful Liver can impede Spleen function, weakening the digestion and distribution of nutrients, which can affect the appetite and lead to food cravings, nausea or fluid retention as the normal circulation systems fail. So as well as Liver *qi* Congestion the PMS sufferer may also have some form of Spleen Deficiency.

Treatments

As well as receiving herbal brews and acupuncture, treatment might include exercise since, in Chinese theory, too much sitting can lead to Congestion and Stagnation. The Spleen can also be weakened by too much cold food so the patient may be advised to eat warm foods and avoid cold drinks or excessive fluid intake since weakened Spleen can lead to Fluid Stagnation and Internal Damp problems.

Chinese herbal treatment for premenstrual syndrome could include remedies to help normalize Liver *qi* and nourish Blood, such as *dang gui* (Chinese angelica), *bai shao yao* (white peony root) or *chai hu* (thorowax root).

Abdominal bloating can be a symptom of premenstrual syndrome.

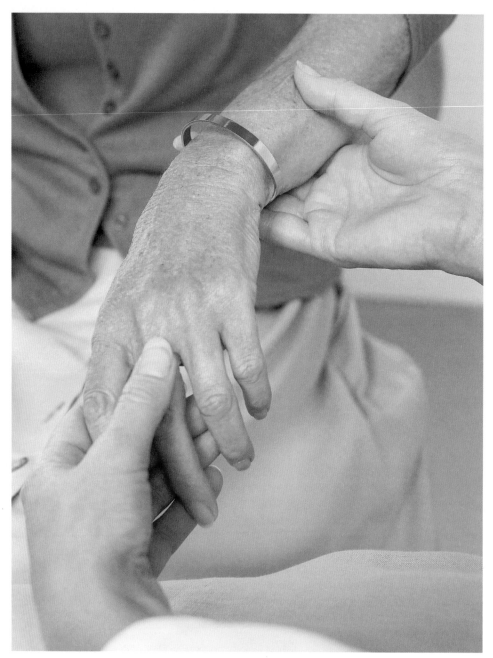

Arthritis, especially rheumatoid arthritis, can affect the joints of the fingers.

ARTHRITIS

Western medicine regards arthritis as a joint inflammation generally treated with anti-inflammatory drugs. There are many types of arthritis including osteoarthritis, caused by wear-and-tear damage to the joints, and rheumatoid arthritis, an auto-immune disease where the body itself destroys the joint lining.

In Chinese theory, arthritis – often referred to as *bi* syndrome – is seen as caused by pathogenic Wind, Cold, Dampness or Heat leading to obstructions of the meridians and sluggish circulation of *qi* and Blood. Symptoms can include numbness and heaviness of the muscles, tendons or joints as well as joint swelling and restricted movement.

Types of bi syndrome

There are various types of *bi* syndrome depending on the invading pathogens and why they have been so successful. Sufferers are likely to have low resistance (weakened *wei qi*) that allows pathogens to enter: those with *yang* Deficiency would be more susceptible to Wind, Cold and Damp; those with *yin* Deficiency or over-dominant *yang* would be more likely to suffer Wind-Heat-Damp *bi* syndrome. In the Wind-Damp-Heat variety joints are red, hot and swollen. If Wind is dominant then the pains shift between joints, if Cold is the predominant pathogen then the

pain is localized and severe, while Dampness increases the sensations of numbness and heaviness.

Initially the problem is seen as exterior and superficial, but if untreated the pathogens enter the interior and the severity increases. Bi syndrome that is fixed rather than producing migratory pains is more akin to the Western definition of rheumatoid arthritis, while the Wind-Cold-Damp variety is more comparable with osteoarthritis.

Treatments

Treatment is focused on expelling the invading pathogens followed by strengthening the Blood and *zang-fu* organs, especially Spleen, Liver and Kidney since these are the organs associated with, respectively, muscles, tendons and bones.

Treatment may also include herbs or acupuncture to encourage Blood circulation and dispel any stasis. Severe Damp can also give rise to Phlegm so, again, if this was present, additional remedies would be used.

Herbs used for the Cold types of arthritis include *ma huang* (ephedra), *gui zhi* (cinnamon twigs), *fang feng* (siler root) and various types of specially prepared aconite (*fu zi*), an extremely toxic plant little used in the West. Tonic remedies like *ren shen* (Korean ginseng) and *huang qi* (milk vetch) may also be added.

HIGH BLOOD PRESSURE

While in the West high blood pressure is generally treated with beta-blockers, vasodilators, diuretics and a host of other pills and potions, Chinese theory focuses on correcting the imbalances that may be causing the condition.

Causes can be:

• emotional problems, with worry affecting the Spleen leading to stagnation of vital energy in the Liver, in turn causing a Flaring of Liver Fire.

• improper diet with too much greasy food and alcohol causing imbalances in Spleen and Stomach, with failure to transport water and nutrients and a resulting increase in Phlegm.

• overwork or ageing with a reduction in Kidney essence that affects the Liver, which in turn causes Flaring of Liver Fire.

Other causes include problems with Phlegm blocking the Heart Channel or Heart Deficiency causing Stagnation of *qi* and Blood.

Symptoms and treatment

The symptoms and treatment of each condition vary significantly. Flaring of Liver Fire, for example, may cause dizziness, headache, blurred vision, a red flushed face, a bitter taste in the mouth, irritability, numbness in lips and tongue, insomnia, with a red tip to the tongue, yellow coating and taut and rapid pulse, as well as raised blood pressure. Treatment focuses on calming the Liver and clearing the endogenous Wind, which is fanning the Fire. Herbs that cool and sedate Liver Fire and clear Heat such as long *dan cao* (gentian), *huang qin baikal* (skullcap root) and *zhi zi* (gardenia fruits) might be included in remedies.

If poor diet has resulted in a build-up of Phlegm, then nausea and vomiting with an oppressive feeling in the stomach, lack of appetite, disturbed and dreamy sleep and a cough with mucous-like sputum might be symptoms. The tongue will still have a red tip but is otherwise pale with a slimy yellow coating and the pulse is taut and slippery. Treatment aims to subdue endogenous Wind but is also focused on clearing Phlegm with warm, drying herbs like *huang lian* (golden thread) and *huang qin baikal* (skullcap root).

If Deficient vital essence of Kidney and Liver is to blame then symptoms may include dizziness, tinnitus, headache, a flushed face on exertion, dry mouth, weight loss, weakness in the lower back and legs, a deep red tongue with little coating and a thready, taut pulse. Here treatment is focused on replenishing vital essence with tonic herbs including *di huang* (Chinese foxglove), *shan zhu yu* (dogwood fruits) or *mu dan pi* (tree peony root bark).

Monitoring their own pressure has become a preoccupation for many people in the West.

DIARRHOEA

While diarrhoea is generally seen in the West as a symptom of food poisoning, irritable bowel syndrome, gastroenteritis or some other disorder, in Chinese theory it can also have a number of other causes and appropriate remedies.

Likely causes

External pathogens are often to blame – Cold, Dampness and Summer Heat are all seen as potential causes of Spleen dysfunction with a failure of the usual mechanisms for transporting and distributing water and nutrients.

There could also be poor Spleen and Stomach function caused by improper diet; too much fatty, sweet, cold, raw or infected food, or emotional strain could be a factor causing stagnation of Liver *qi* that damages the Spleen. In chronic illness, too, Kidney *qi* can be weakened, which in turn fails to strengthen the Spleen.

Diagnosis

Diagnosis includes examining the precise pattern of the diarrhoea and stools: loose, watery stools with indigestion suggests pathogenic Cold; stools that are dark and smell particularly unpleasant accompanied by a burning sensation in the anus suggest pathogenic Heat.

Treatments

The aim of treatment is to clear the pathogen with supportive herbs: warm, drying remedies in the case of pathogenic Cold and cool, and often bitter tasting herbs if Heat is to blame.

Diarrhoea owing to Spleen weakness generally involves undigested food in the stool due to a failure of the digestive system. Weak Spleen may also involve lack of appetite, lethargy, a feeling of oppression in the area around the stomach. The tongue will be pale with a white coating and the pulse weak and thready. Here treatment is aimed at reinforcing the Spleen's vital energy using tonic herbs such as *dang shen* (bellflower root) and remedies to clear Damp and normalize function like the fungus *fu ling* (tuckahoe).

If Kidney weakness is to blame, then the condition generally manifests as 'cock-crow diarrhoea' in the early morning with abdominal pains relieved when passing stools, and often cold limbs, lower back pain and weak knees. The tongue is pale with a white coating and the pulse deep and thready. Treatment aims to strengthen both Kidney and Spleen.

A classic herbal remedy in this case is *si shen wan* ('pills of four miraculous drugs') that contains *bu gu zi* (scuffy pea seeds), *wu zhu yu* (evodia fruits), *rou dou kou* (nutmeg) and *wu wei zi* (schizandra fruits).

'Cock-crow diarrhoea' is typified by an early morning rush for the bathroom with abdominal pain that is soon relieved.

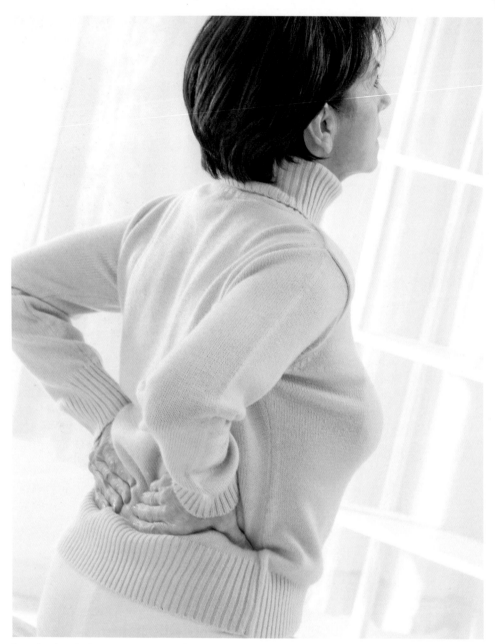

Low back pain is a common complaint that Western medicine sees as a mechanical problem.

LOW BACK PAIN OR LUMBAGO

Backache is one of those common ailments that affects many people. In Western medicine a mechanical cause is generally sought – as wear-and-tear on vertebra, misaligned discs, sprained muscles, or trapped nerves; urinary tract, kidney or fallopian tube inflammations may also be blamed.

Symptoms and treatment

In Chinese theory there are also several possible causes of low back pain. It could be caused by Damp-Cold entering the lumbar region and impairing the smooth flow of *qi* and Blood. Typically, there is increased pain on cold, wet days that is not relieved by bed rest, although the pain is relieved by warmth in the lumbar region. There is a slimy white coating to the tongue and deep slow pulse. Treatment is aimed at clearing the Cold and Damp and improving *qi* and Blood flow with herbs such as *fu ling* (tuckahoe), *bai zhu* (white atractylodes) and *du huo* (pubescent angelica).

Low back pain could also be related to Damp-Heat – both exogenous or endogenous – entering the Channels and causing obstructions. Symptoms include pain with a burning sensation and a bitter taste in the mouth. The tongue has a slimy yellow coating and the pulse is soft and rapid. Treatment is with cooling, dry herbs such as *huang bai* (cork tree bark) and *yi yi ren* (Job's tears seeds).

The pain may be related to weakened Kidney *jing*, possibly associated with the normal run-down of essence in old age or excessive sexual activity. Pain may be relieved by pressure; symptoms could also include weakness in the legs and knees, dizziness, tinnitus, cold limbs and a pale tongue with white coating and a deep, thready pulse. Tonic herbs for the Kidney in this case are *gou qi zi* (wolfberry fruits) and *shan zhu yu* (dogwood fruits).

Finally, low back pain may be related to *qi* and Blood Stagnation caused by traumatic injury or chronic illness. The pain is likely to be sharp and stinging and is made worse by movement and pressure. The tongue will be dark red with a choppy pulse. Treatment is designed to normalize the Blood circulation and remove Blood Stagnation. Typical herbal remedies will include *dang gui* (Chinese angelica), *chuan xiong* (Szechuan lovage) and *hong hua* (safflower).

CHINESE
MATERIA MEDICA

TYPES OF CHINESE HERBAL REMEDIES

Herbal remedies form the basis of traditional Chinese therapeutics: while acupuncture or massage are seen by many Westerners as more significant therapies, herbs will be prescribed in almost all cases and are regarded as the physician's most important tool. Herbs in Chinese theory can also include far more than plants: animal parts, minerals, fungi, human hair, insects, or even various animal droppings have all been used as medicine over the centuries.

The earliest herbal, the *Shen Nong Ben Cao Jing* (*The Divine Farmer's Herb Classic*) was written around CE 200, although it is believed to have existed in oral tradition for several thousand *years* before that. It lists 365 herbs including many that are still in use today. *Ma huang* (ephedra), for example, is still used to treat asthma and gave us the drug ephedrine, while the classic text refers to *dang gui* (Chinese angelica) as suitable for regulating menstruation: it is now sold as an over-the-counter remedy in Western shops for this very purpose.

HERBAL CATEGORIES

Over the centuries, Chinese scholars identified more healing remedies; the renowned Li Shi Zhen publishing his *Ben Cao Gan Mu* in the 1590s with its impressive listings of some 1,892 remedies made up into more

than 11,000 different combinations. The remedies are grouped into such categories as woods, weeds, fruits and so on, and listed by the Mandarin Chinese name for each 'drug'.

Western *materia medica* are very precise in identifying the individual plants by standard botanical name but China is a large country and many of the plants growing in the sub-tropical south are very different from those growing in the cooler north. Different plants from the various regions may have similar therapeutic properties and be used in the same way, so it is possible for several unrelated botanical species to share the same Mandarin 'drug' name.

This can seem confusing. Two quite different species of duckweed, for example, (*Spirodela polyrrhiza* and *Lemma minor*) are both called *fu ping* and used to treat common colds caused by Wind and Heat. Similarly,

The complete Chinese 'herbal' repertoire includes shells, insects, minerals and animal parts.

fang ji – a pungent remedy used to relieve the pain caused by Wind and Dampness in rheumatic and arthritic disorders — can be derived from *Stephania*, *Aristolochia* or *Cocculus* species. *Aristolochia* species are highly toxic and can be fatal if misused so in restricting the use of *fang ji*, Western regulators also deny access to other safer remedies.

NAMING DIFFERENT PARTS

Equally confusing for non-Mandarin speakers is that different parts of the same plant can also have quite different Chinese names: cinnamon, for example, can be either *gui zhi* (twigs) or *rou gui* (bark); rather simpler is the white mulberry tree (*Morus alba*), which gives rise to *sang bai pi* (bark), *sang zhi* (twigs), *sang shen* (fruit) and *sang ye* (leaves), *sang pia xiao* is the steamed and dried egg case of the praying mantis laid on mulberry leaves, used to replenish Kidney *yang*, while *sang ji sheng* is mulberry mistletoe.

DIFFERENT PROCESSES

Plants can also be processed in different ways giving rise to further naming combinations: *di huang* is the root of the Chinese foxglove while *sheng di huang* is the fresh or dried root and *shu di huang* is a cooked or 'prepared' version.

DIFFERENT COMBINATIONS

While Western herbalists tend to mix different plant extracts together on an *ad hoc* basis to treat each individual patient, Chinese medicine details many thousands of standard formulae that are used as the basis of prescribing. Traditional Chinese medicine practitioners know hundreds of these combinations by heart and may use the basic combination, or amend it very slightly for their patients. The same formulations are also sold as ready-made products, some of which are available as over-the-counter remedies in the West.

The herbs in each prescription play quite different roles. These include:

• The emperor or chief — the principal therapeutic herb

• Ministers or deputies — herbs that support/strengthen the key plants

• A messenger or assistant — based on the directional properties of the plant this 'targets' the prescription to particular meridians or parts of the body

• ambassadors, helpers or harmonizers — auxiliary and/or correcting herbs that counter any toxic effects of the major ingredients or deal with secondary symptoms in the condition.

All parts of the white mulberry tree are used in Chinese medicine.

HERBAL REMEDIES

The properties of herbs used in traditional Chinese medicine reflect the various theories of five elements, *yin-yang* and meridians.

All herbal plants are defined in terms of their property and taste. Herbs are also described as entering the meridians and have a direction inside the body with *yang* herbs tending to move upwards and *yin* downwards. Each attribute signifies further actions. Bitter herbs, for example, will reverse the upward flow of *qi* while hot herbs dispel pathogenic Cold and strengthen *yang*.

Using this directory

Traditional Chinese herbals tended to group plants either by type of remedy or by therapeutic action. Since Chinese names mean very little to Western readers, the listings in this section adopt this approach and group herbs by main action.

Each is given with its three names – Western, Chinese and botanical – and basic characteristics. These include the herb's taste, associated meridians and its actions. There is also advice on how to use it and for which medical conditions.

PROPERTIES OF HERBS AND ASSOCIATED SYNDROMES

Property	Action	Used for
Cold (*han*)/ cool (*liang*)	To clear Heat	Heart pain, palpitations, insomnia, night sweats
Warm (*wen*)/ hot (*re*)	To purge Fire	Deafness, lower abdominal pain and distention
Neutral (*ping*)	To remove Toxins	Heat syndromes

TASTES OF HERBS AND ASSOCIATED SYNDROMES

Taste	Action	Used for
Pungent (la)	Dispersing/mobilizing	Superficial syndrome Wind syndrome Stagnant *qi* syndrome Stagnant Blood syndrome
Sour (suan), astringent	Contracting	Sweating associated with Deficiency Haemorrhage due to Deficiency Chronic diarrhoea Involuntary urination
Sweet (gan)	Tonifying Clearing toxins Alleviating Harmonizing the action of drugs	*Yin, yang* or *qi* Deficient syndromes Spasmodic pain
Salty (xian)	Softening/eliminating Lubricating the large intestine	Combating swellings (in lymphatic system) and other masses Constipation
Bitter (ku)	Reversing upward motion of *qi* Drying Damp evil Activating *qi* and Blood motion	Coughs, vomiting, constipation due to stagnation, problems with urination Water-Damp syndromes Coughs due to stagnant Lung *qi*, Stagnant Blood syndromes
Bland	Diuresis	Water-Damp syndromes

TAKING HERBAL REMEDIES

Traditionally, most Chinese herbal remedies are made into decoctions known as *tang* (soup). Patients are given small paper bags containing each day's dosage; this is soaked with three cups of water (about 500 ml) for about 20–30 minutes, then simmered gently until the volume has reduced by about half (another 25–30 minutes). This mixture is then strained and the liquid is taken as a single dose on an empty stomach.

The quantities of herbs one might use each day are generally higher than quantities found in forms of Western herbal medicine and, as a result, Chinese decoctions are usually a thick, dark brown with a strong, generally unpleasant taste that many Westerners find difficult to take.

As well as decoctions, Chinese herbal formulae can also be powdered (*san*) or made into pills (*wan*). Pills, usually resembling small black ball bearings, are traditionally made by rolling powdered herbs with honey, and dosages are generally around six or eight pills at a time. Powders are generally stirred into water or wine.

Some prescriptions are specifically designed to be taken in pill form – such as *liu wei di huang wan* (pills of six ingredients with Chinese foxglove) taken for Liver and Kidney *yin* Deficiency.

Herbal wines (*jiu*) are also used as tonic remedies with roots simply steeped in wine for several weeks and then taken in small doses on a daily basis.

ADAPTING TO WESTERN LIFESTYLES

Brewing the daily *tang* is a time-consuming business for Western households; consequently, Western-trained acupuncturists and many practitioners working in the West use alternative extracts.

Commercial producers now supply many of the traditional *tang* formulae in capsules, tablets or as liquid extracts. These are easy, convenient and pleasant to take, although some purists would argue that they are not as always as effective as the traditional remedies.

Long-standing tradition

In recent years, a market has developed for over-the-counter Chinese herbs for use in non-traditional ways. Individual herbs are often available in tincture or fluid extract form in health food shops, while various blends of herbal powders or liquid extracts are sold under a variety of names. They are designed to appeal to Western shoppers, who buy them in much the same way as they might by vitamin or mineral supplements. Many of these bear little resemblance to traditional Chinese herbal preparations.

It has to be said that, applied conventionally, traditional Chinese herbal medicine very rarely uses a single herb as a remedy; the emphasis is always on tried-and-trusted formulae that have evolved over the centuries. So taking single herbs in the way described above is most unusual.

Equally, while it is true that a number of different herbs might be added to a standard formula in order to adapt a certain mix to a particular medical condition or syndrome, such formulae are also well-defined. These are standardized combinations that share little of the *ad hoc* approach to herbal remedies that are common in the Western world.

Chinese herbal preparations – soups, pills and powders – have been made in much the same way for generations.

HERBS FOR EXTERIOR CONDITIONS

Exterior or superficial diseases (see pages 48–55) are caused by external 'evils' such as Cold, Damp or Wind-Heat. Typical symptoms include coughs, chills, fevers or general muscle aches regarded in the West as typical of the 'common cold'. The herbs used to treat these conditions are described as 'releasing the exterior'. Herbs for Exterior conditions fall into two main groups — warm pungent herbs, used for treating Cold conditions, and cold pungent herbs, used for treating Heat problems.

WARM PUNGENT HERBS

Warm pungent herbs are used where the chills are severe, fever is mild and additional symptoms might include headache, body and neck pains and a lack of thirst.

Cinnamon twigs

Chinese name
Gui zhi

Botanical name
Cinnamomum cassia

Taste Pungent, sweet

Character Warm

Meridians Heart, Lung, Urinary Bladder

Actions Antibacterial, antifungal, antiviral, analgesic, carminative, cardiotonic, diuretic.

The twigs of Chinese cinnamon are a popular remedy for treating external Cold and Wind-Cold conditions. It is said to 'warm the channels' and is included in prescriptions for some gynecological problems such as period pain associated with internal Cold. As a warming herb it is naturally *yang* and is used to improve the circulation of *yang qi* and strengthen Heart *yang*.

Applications For Exterior Cold it can be taken in teas and is often combined with *bai shao yao* (white peony), *sheng jiang* (fresh ginger) and *gan cao* (baked liquorice).

⊗ *Gui zhi* should be avoided in feverish conditions, excess Heat or Fire, and in pregnancy.

Perilla leaf

Chopped cinnamon twigs

Perilla leaf

Chinese name
Zi su ye

Botanical name
Perilla frutescens

Taste Pungent

Character Warm

Meridians Lung, Spleen

Actions Antibacterial, antitussive (anticoughing), diaphoretic (antiperspiring), expectorant

Perilla is a familiar herb in the West, where it is commonly used as an ingredient in Chinese and Japanese cookery.

In Chinese medicine, the leaves are used to disperse Exterior Cold, especially Wind-Cold with coughs, and also to circulate Stomach and Spleen *qi* associated with *san jiao* disharmony. Perilla seeds are mostly used as a cough remedy to clear Phlegm.

Applications For Wind-Cold it can be taken in teas with *jie geng* (balloon flower) and is also made into a powder as *xiang su san*, which contains *chen pi* (tangerine peel), *xiang fu* (cyperus) and *gan cao* (baked liquorice).

⊗ *Zi su ye* should be avoided for feverish diseases and *qi* Deficiency.

Fresh ginger root

Fresh ginger root

Chinese name *Sheng jiang*

Botanical name *Zingiber officinale*

Taste Pungent

Character Warm

Meridians Lung, Spleen, Stomach

Actions Antiemetic, antispasmodic, antiseptic, carminative, circulatory stimulant, diaphoretic, expectorant, peripheral vasodilator, topically: rubefacient

Widely used both as a remedy in its own right and cooked with other herbs to reduce their toxicity, *sheng jiang* (fresh ginger) is used as a warming remedy for Wind-Cold.

Ginger root is said to strengthen the *wei qi* and 'release the Exterior'. It also warms the middle *jiao* and is used for vomiting associated with Cold in the Stomach. Dried ginger (*gan jiang*) is a more warming remedy while the peel of fresh ginger root (*sheng jiang pi*) is used as a diuretic.

Applications For Wind-Cold *sheng jiang* is generally decocted with a little brown sugar added.

⊗ Avoid *sheng jiang* in Internal Heat syndromes.

Other warm pungent herbs

- **Notopterygii root** (*qing huo*; *Notopterygium incisium*): commonly used when the condition also involves Dampness.

- **Siler root** (*fang feng*; *Ledebouriella sesloides*): mainly used for Wind-Cold and Wind-Damp linked to rheumatic disorders.

- **Dahurian angelica** (*bai zhi*; *Angelica dahurica*): mainly used to expel Wind.

- **Wild ginger** (*xi xin*; *Asarum sieba*ldi): used to warm the Lungs and expel Cold and Wind.

- **Magnolia flower** (*xin yi hua*; *Magnolia liliflora*): used to expel Wind and open the nasal passages.

COOL PUNGENT HERBS

These are used for Wind-Heat superficial syndromes where symptoms include relatively severe fevers with chills, dry or sore throat, and thirst. Some can also be used for eye problems associated with Wind-Heat.

Field mint

Chinese name *Bo he*

Botanical name *Mentha arvensis*

Taste Pungent

Character Cool

Meridians Liver, Lung

Actions Antibacterial, antiinflammatory, antispasmodic, analgesic, diaphoretic to disperse Stagnant Liver *qi*.

A key remedy for Wind-Heat problems especially where symptoms include headache and sore throat, field mint 'let outs' skin eruptions so is used for measles and other rashes. It helps to disperse Stagnant Liver *qi*.

Applications For Wind-Heat use with *niu bang zi* (burdock seeds) or combine with *lian qi*ao (forsythia fruits) and *jin yin hua* (honeysuckle flowers). For Stagnant Liver *qi* a small amount is included in formulae containing *bai shao yao* (white peony) or *chai hu* (thorowax root).

⊗ *Bo he* should be avoided in *yin* Deficiency and Excess Liver *qi*.

Field mint

Chrysanthemum flowers

Chinese name *Ju hua*

Botanical name *Dendranthema x grandiflorum*

Taste Pungent, sweet, bitter

Character Cool

Meridians Lung, Liver

Actions Antibacterial, antifungal, antiviral, antiinflammatory, hypotensive, peripheral vasodilator

Chrysanthemum flowers

One of China's most popular over-the-counter herbal teas, chrysanthemum flowers are generally steamed before being dried, which removes much of the bitterness.

Ju hua is used to clear pathogenic Wind-Heat and also used to clear Liver Heat. Since the Liver is associated with the eyes *ju hua* eases sore red eyes when caused either by Wind-Heat in the Liver Channel or Liver Fire.

Applications *Ju hua* is often used with *sang ye* (mulberry leaf) for pathogenic Heat affecting the upper *jiao* and with *shu di huang* (Chinese foxglove), *gou qi zi* (wolfberry fruits) or *bao shao yao* (white peony) for eye problems.

⊗ *Ju hua* should be avoided in diarrhoea and *qi* Deficiency.

Thorowax root

Chinese name *Chai hu*

Botanical name *Bupleurum chinense*

Taste Bitter, pungent

Character Slightly cold

Meridians Liver, Gall bladder, Pericardium, *san jiao*

Actions Antibacterial, antiviral, antimalarial, analgesic, antiinflammatory, cholagogue, mild hypotensive, sedative

One of the herbs commonly used in China to treat malaria, thorowax root is regarded as a remedy for pathogenic Wind-Heat, and an important treatment for dispersing stagnant Liver *qi* associated with gynecological disorders.

Applications To disperse external evils that have entered the *shaoyang* Channel and becoming a more serious Internal problem. It is often combined with *huang qin baikal* (skullcap root), *ban xia* (pinellia), and *gan cao* (liquorice). For stagnant Liver *qi* it is commonly used with *bai shao yao* (white peony), *dang gui* (Chinese angelica) and *fu ling* (tuckahoe).

⊗ *Chai hu* should be avoided in Liver Fire or *yin* Deficiency.

Other cold pungent herbs

- **Burdock seed** (*niu bang zi* ; *Arctium lappa*): mainly used for dispersing Wind-Heat and associated skin eruptions.

- **Mulberry leaf** (*sang ye*; *Morus alba*): used to expel Wind and clear Heat from the Lungs; also used for Heat or Wind in the Liver Channel causing eye problems.

- **Kudzu vine root** (*ge gen*; *Pueraria lobata*): used to disperse pathogenic Wind-Heat and Wind-Cold and also to increase Spleen and Stomach *qi* where symptoms can include diarrhoea.

- **Duckweed** (*fu ping*; *Spirodela polyrrhiza* or *Lemna minor*): one of the few cold and pungent herbs that is also diaphoretic; used for common colds, Wind rash and measles.

Sliced thorowax root

HERBS TO CLEAR HEAT

Heat can be an External and Internal problem. Typical Heat symptoms include dry throat, red face or eyes, dark and scanty urine, dry stools, a rapid pulse and yellow coating to the tongue. External Heat problems may include fever and chills, while Internal Heat is more likely to cause thirst, irritability and feeling hot but without a chill or cold. Herbs to clear Internal Heat are all cold and often have a bitter taste. They are divided into five groups of herbs to: quell Fire; cool Blood; clear Heat and dry Dampness; clear Heat and Poisons; clear Summer Heat.

HERBS TO QUELL FIRE

These are some of the coldest herbs in the repertoire and are used for treating high fevers and heat in the Liver, Lungs and Stomach. In Western terms they are known to be antimicrobial, anti-inflammatory and antipyretic.

Gypsum

Chinese name *Shi gao*

Chemical name *Calcium sulphate* (often naturally occurring with iron or magnesium salts)

Taste Sweet, pungent

Character Cold

Meridians Lung, Stomach

Actions Antipyretic, sedative, decreases the permeability of blood vessels, inhibits sweating, increases blood calcium levels

Gypsum is added to a herbal mixture as small broken pieces of rock. *Shi gao* is also used to clear excess Heat from the Lungs, characterized by coughing and wheezing; and also controls Stomach Fire that can cause toothache, painful gums or headache.

Applications With *shu di huang* (prepared Chinese foxglove) for headaches and toothaches caused by Internal Fire.

⊗ *Shi gao* should not be used in Deficient *yang* syndromes, where the Stomach is weak or if there are no signs of Heat or Dampness.

Anemarrhena root

Chinese name *Zhi mu*

Botanical name *Anemarrhena asphodeloides*

Taste Bitter

Character Cold

Meridians Lung, Stomach, Kidney

Actions Antibacterial, diuretic, hypoglycemic, expectorant, antifungal, antipyretic

Anemarrhena root is widely used to reduce Heat and quell Fire as well as to nurture *yin* and moisten Dry conditions.

Applications *Zhi mu* is for conditions involving Heat and *yin* Deficiency. It is used in *er mu san* (fritillary and anemarrhena powder) for menopausal problems or in *gui zhi shao yao zhi mu tang* (decoction of cinnamon twig, peony and anemarrhena) for certain types of arthritis. It is used with *xuan shen* (Ningpo figwort) and *sheng di huang* (Chinese foxglove) for mouth ulcers.

⊗ Avoid using *zhi mu* if symptoms include diarrhoea.

Sliced anemarrhena root

Other herbs to quell Fire

- **Self-heal flower** (*xia ku cao*; *Prunella vulgaris*): Spikes used mainly for treating Liver Fire.

- **Gardenia fruit** (*zhi zi*; *Gardenia jasminoides*): used to drain Heat from the *san jiao*.

- **Reed rhizome** (*lu gen*; *Phragmites communis*) used to clear Heat from Lungs and Stomach and generate Fluids.

Fresh self-heal flowers

HERBS THAT COOL BLOOD

Symptoms associated with Heat in the Blood include rashes, spitting or vomiting blood, nosebleeds, and blood in the urine or stool.

Chinese foxglove root (fresh or dried)

Chinese name *Sheng di huang*

Botanical name *Rehmannia glutinosa*

Taste Sweet, bitter

Character Cold

Meridians Heart, Liver, Kidney

Actions Antibacterial, antifungal, diuretic, hypertensive, increases coagulation.

Young Chinese foxglove plant

Chinese foxglove is used as either fresh or dried root (*sheng di huang*) and a cooked form made by stir-frying the sliced tubers in wine (*shu di huang*).

Sheng *di huang* is used to clear Heat, cool the Blood, nourish *yin* and generate body fluids. It also 'cools the upward flaring of Heart Fire' that can cause mouth and tongue sores and lead to insomnia and irritability. S*hu di huang* is an important Blood tonic.

Applications *Sheng di huang* is combined with other cold herbs, such as *xuan shen ningpo* (figwort) or *mu dan pi* (tree peony root bark) for treating feverish diseases that may be affecting Blood. With herbs such as *qing hao* (sweet wormwood) and *mu dan pi* it is used for *yin* Deficiency in the later stages of fevers.

⊗ Both forms of *di huang* should be avoided if there is diarrhoea; *sheng di huang* should not be taken if there is Deficient *yang* or Spleen and is best avoided in pregnancy.

Figwort root

Chinese name *Xuan shen ningpo*

Botanical name *Scrophularia ningpoensis*

Taste Bitter, salty

Character Cold

Meridians Lung, Stomach, Kidney

Actions Antibacterial, antiviral, cardiotonic, hypotensive, hypoglycemic

Figwort root

Figwort root is used for clearing pathogenic Heat that has entered the Blood and to nourish *yin*, it is particularly effective for dispelling nodules and detoxifying Fire Poisons.

Applications *Xuan shen* combines well with *lian qiao* (forsythia fruits) for deep-seated abscesses and with *niu bang zi* (burdock seeds) for acute swellings in the throat. For irritant rashes it works well with *mu dan pi* (tree peony root bark).

⊗ *Xuan shen* should be avoided if symptoms include diarrhoea.

Other herbs to cool Blood

- **Tree peony root bark** (*mu dan pi*; *Paeonia suffruticosa*): helps to invigorate Blood to clear Stagnation and congealed masses, and helps to clear ascending Liver fire.

- **Wolfberry root bark** (*di gu pi*; *Lycium chinense*): used to clear Deficient *yin* Fire and Heat.

HERBS TO CLEAR HEAT AND DRY DAMPNESS

Mainly used for Damp-Heat syndromes with symptoms that include problems with urination, diarrhoea, eczema or jaundice, these herbs are mostly cold and bitter and in conventional medical terms would be described as anti-inflammatory and antipyretic.

Skullcap root

Chinese name *Huang qin baikal*

Botanical name *Scutellaria baicalensis*

Taste Bitter

Character Cold

Meridians Lung, Heart, Stomach, Gall Bladder, Large Intestine

Actions Antibacterial, antispasmodic, diuretic, febrifuge, lowers blood cholesterol

This is mainly used to clear Damp-Heat and quell Fire, especially in the upper *jiao*, it also is said to 'calm the foetus and pacify the womb' in conditions where the foetus is over-active and kicking due to Heat.

Applications *Huang qin* is generally used with other cooling herbs like *huang lian* (Chinese golden thread) and *xuan shen ningpo* (figwort) for feverish conditions with dry throat, insomnia, diarrhoea, boils or acute infections. It is used with *xia ku cao* (self-heal spikes) for excess Liver

Fire and with remedies like *mu dan pi* (tree peony root bark) or *sheng di huang* (Chinese foxglove) where there is Heat in the Blood.

⊗ Avoid *huang qin* where there are no true Heat and Dampness symptoms.

Skullcap root

Cork tree

Chinese name *Huang bai*

Botanical name *Phellodendron amurense*

Taste Bitter

Character Cold

Meridians Kidney, Urinary Bladder

Actions Antibacterial, cholagogue, diuretic, hypoglycemic, hypotensive, antipyretic

Cork tree bark

Huang bai is particularly effective for Damp-Heat in the lower *jiao* and is also used to quell Kidney Fire and drain Fire Poisons causing sores and skin lesions.

Applications *Huang bai* is combined with *shan yao* (Chinese yam) for urinary problems associated with Damp-Heat and with *chi shao yao* (red peony) where there is also Heat in the Blood. It is included in patent remedies including *er miao san* (powder of two effective ingredients) used to clear Heat and Dampness and *zhi bai di huang wan* (anemarrhena, cork tree and pills of six herbs with Chinese foxglove) to replenish Kidney *yin*.

⊗ *Huang bai* should be avoided if there is diarrhoea or Stomach weakness.

Other herbs to clear Heat and dry Dampness

- **Gold thread root** (*huang lian*; *Coptis chinensis*): used for a wide range of Heat problems including dysentery, 'marauding Hot Blood', excess Stomach Heat, mouth ulceration, boils and abscesses.

- **Chinese gentian root** (*Long dan cao*; *Gentiana scabra*): used to drain Heat and Damp from the Liver and Gall Bladder Channels associated with red and swollen throat, eyes and ears as well as to calm Liver Fire.

HERBS THAT CLEAR HEAT AND POISONS

Hot Poisons (*re du*) and Fire Poisons (*huodu*) are typified by fevers, swellings, abscesses and dysentery. These herbs are all cooling and most are known to be anti-inflammatory, antimicrobial or antiviral.

Honeysuckle flowers

Chinese name *Jin yin hua*

Botanical name *Lonicera japonica*

Taste Sweet

Character Cold

Meridians Lung, Stomach, Large Intestine

Actions Antibacterial, antiviral, hypotensive

Honeysuckle flowers

Jin yin hua means 'gold silver flower' and the herb is used for superficial Wind-Heat conditions as well as internal disorders related to Damp-Heat in the lower *jiao* and Fire Poisons causing swellings especially in the breast, throat or eyes.

Applications *Jin yin hua* is used with herbs like *jing jie* (schizonepeta) and *bo he* (field mint) for External Wind-Heat or with *huang qin baikal* (skullcap) for feverish conditions. With *jie geng* (balloon flower) and *nui bang zi* (burdock seeds) it is used for pain and swelling in the throat.

⊗ *Jin yin hua* should be avoided in Deficient and Cold conditions.

Forsythia fruits

Chinese name *Lian qiao*

Botanical name *Forsythia suspensa*

Taste Bitter

Character Slightly cold

Meridians Lung, Heart, Gall Bladder

Actions Antibacterial, antiemetic, antiparasitic

Lian qiao is effective at clearing External Heat and deeper-seated Fire Poisons causing abscesses, sores and swellings. It is used for feverish colds with sore throats and headaches, for infections involving swollen neck glands or lymph nodes, and for urinary tract infections.

Applications For external Heat problems *Lian qiao* is often used with *niu bang zi* (burdock seeds), *jing jie* (schizonepeta) and *bo he* (field mint); for internal problems — skin rashes and abscesses —combine with *mu dan pi* (tree peony root bark), *chi shao yao* (red peony) or *xuan shen ningpo* (figwort root).

⊗ Avoid *lian qiao* in diarrhoea associated with Deficient Spleen, fevers linked to Deficient *qi* and purulent abscesses.

HERBS THAT CLEAR SUMMER HEAT

Summer heat is a seasonal disorder typified by fever, irritability, thirst and diarrhoea.

Sweet wormwood

Chinese name *Qing hao*

Botanical name *Artemisia annua*

Taste Bitter

Character Cold

Meridians Liver, Gall Bladder

Actions Antibacterial, antifungal, antimalarial

Sweet wormwood is regarded by many as a low cost antimalarial remedy. It is used for cooling Blood, clearing fevers associated with Deficient Blood, and reducing Heat associated with Deficient *yin*.

Applications *Qing hao* has been used on is own in doses of up to 40g for malaria. It is combined with *sheng di huang* (Chinese foxglove) and *mu dan pi* (tree peony root bark) for Heat associated with Deficient yin.

⊗ Avoid in diarrhoea or if there are no signs of Heat due to Deficient *yin*.

DOWNWARD DRAINING HERBS

Herbs in this group can be described as moist laxatives, purgative and cathartics. They all stimulate or lubricate the gastro-intestinal tract to encourage defecation. Purgatives are used for Interior Excess syndromes including constipation caused by Excess Heat or pathogenic Cold. Moist laxatives lubricate the intestines and are used where constipation is associated with Deficient Blood, *yin* or *qi*. Cathartics are powerful remedies used where constipation is associated with Stagnation of Fluid or poor water metabolism. They can damage *yin* and *qi* if misused and should only be used by qualified practitioners.

Chinese rhubarb root

Chinese name *Da huang*

Botanical name *Rheum palmatum*

Taste Bitter

Character Cold

Meridians Liver, Spleen, Stomach, Large Intestine

Actions Purgative, antibacterial, antifungal, antiparasitic, hypotensive, lowers blood cholesterol levels, cholagogue, diuretic, haemostatic

Rhubarb root is an important herb in the purgative category. It is used for constipation associated with pathogenic Heat, and for dysentery-like disorders related to Damp Heat. It also invigorates Blood and clears Fire Poisons.

Applications *Da huang* can be used with *rou gou* (cinnamon bark) for constipation or with *huang lian* (Chinese golden thread) and *huang qin baikal* (skullcap root) for abdominal bloating associated with Heat or nosebleeds and vomiting blood due to Marauding Hot Blood. It is made into a paste with *shi gao* (gypsum) for burns.

⊗ Avoid *da huang* where there are no Heat or Fire symptoms.

Hemp seeds

Hemp seeds

Chinese name *Huo ma ren*

Botanical name *Cannabis sativa*

Taste Sweet

Character Neutral

Meridians Spleen, Stomach, Large Intestine

Actions Laxative, hypotensive

Cannabis seeds are used as a moist laxative in Chinese medicine. They moisten the Intestines and nourish *yin*. Deficient *yin* can be a cause of constipation in the elderly or after feverish illnesses. Cannabis seeds also clear Heat and encourage healing of sores so are often added to remedies for ulceration or applied topically.

Applications *Huo ma ren* is combined with *dang gui* (Chinese angelica) for constipation in the elderly or after childbirth. It is sometimes combined with herbs such as *jin yin hua* (honeysuckle flowers) and *gan cao* (liquorice) for problems associated with Stomach Heat.

⊗ Avoid cannabis seeds if symptoms include diarrhoea.

Other purgative herbs

- **Senna leaf** (*fan zi e ye*; *Cassia angustifolia*): used to clear excess Heat especially in habitual constipation; it should be avoided in pregnancy.

- **Aloe juice** (*lu hui*; *Aloe vera*): purges Heat from the Liver and Large Intestine and is used where symptoms include headache, dizziness and tinnitus.

HERBS TO CLEAR DAMPNESS

In Chinese medicine 'dampness' can mean excess fluid in the body or suggest a Damp-Heat problem such as 'Damp Warm Febrile diseases' or purulent rashes. Herbs used to drain Dampness are diuretic — increasing urination — in conventional medicine.

Tuckahoe or Indian bread fungus

Chinese name *Fu ling*

Botanical name *Poria cocos*

Taste Sweet, neutral

Character Neutral

Meridians Lung, Spleen, Heart, Urinary Bladder

Actions Diuretic, sedative, hypoglycemic

Fu ling has been used as a diuretic for Dampness and Phlegm since the days of Shen Nong. While the whole sclerotium is known as *fu ling*, the skin is separated as *fu ling pi* and used as a diuretic while the central part of the sclerotium is *fu shen* used as a calming remedy for the Heart.

Applications *Fu ling* is combined with *gui zhi* (cinnamon twigs) and *bai zhu* (white atractylodes) and *ze xie* (water plantain) for Damp-Heat

conditions such as Painful Urinary Dysfunction or with *ban xia* (pinellia) and *chen pi* (tangerine peel) for Congested Fluid syndromes with vomiting and loss of appetite.

⊗ Avoid *fu ling* in excessive urination or prolapse of the urogenital organs.

Tuckahoe

Akebia stems

Chinese name *Mu tong*

Botanical name *Akebia trifoliata*

Taste Bitter

Character Cool

Meridians Heart, Small Intestine, Urinary Bladder

Actions Antibacterial, antifungal, diuretic, antitumour, antiinflammatory, analgesic, immune stimulant

Until the 17th century *mu tong* was generally sourced from akebia species, but in the 1950s the commonest source came from *Aristolochia manshuriensis*, which is rich in aristolochic acid and is now known to cause kidney failure. As such *mu tong* became discredited. Today, akebia is once again being used for *mu tong* as is *Clematis montana*. The herb is mainly used as a diuretic in urinary conditions. Several traditional formulae containing *mu tong* have been modified by suppliers to avoid the herb, although as the stems of *Clematis montana* (a common garden climber) make a suitable substitute safe alternatives should be readily available.

Applications *Mu tong* is included in several patent remedies including long dan *xie gan tang* (decoction to purge the Liver Fire with gentian), with *huang qi* (milk vetch) and *dang gui* (Chinese angelica) for poor milk flow in breast-feeding associated with Deficient *qi*. It is used with *huai niu xi* (ox knee root) and *hong hua* (safflower) for menstrual problems associated with Congealed Blood.

⊗ Avoid in pregnancy or if there is frequent urination.

Fresh akebia plant

Water plantain rhizome

Chinese name *Ze xie*

Botanical name *Alisma plantago-aquatica*

Taste Sweet

Character Cold

Meridians Kidney, Urinary Bladder

Actions Diuretic, hypotensive, anti-bacterial. hypoglycemic

Water plantain rhizomes

Water plantain is an effective diuretic used for problems associated with Excess Dampness.

It also drains Kidney Fire so is used for Deficient Kidney *yin* associated with excess Heat where symptoms can include dizziness and tinnitus.

Dried pinks

Applications *Ze xie* is used in *fu ling ze xie tang* (tuckahoe and plantain decoction), which also contains *gui zhi* (cinnamon twigs) and *sheng jiang* (fresh ginger) and is used to clear Dampness in the Stomach; or in *liu wei di huang* (pills of six ingredients with Chinese foxglove) used to strengthen Kidney and Liver *yin*.

⊗ Avoid *ze xie* in seminal emissions associated with Deficient Kidney *yang* or Damp-Cold.

Pinks

Chinese name *Qu mai*

Botanical name *Dianthus superbus or D. chinensis*

Taste Bitter

Character Cold

Meridians Heart, Kidney, Small Intestine, Urinary Bladder

Actions Diuretic, hypotensive, anti-bacterial

Qu mai is one of the original herbs listed by Shen Nong. It is used for constipation as well as to increase urination. It clears Damp Heat and is also used for menstrual problems associated with Congealed Blood.

Applications *Qu mai* is used with *hua shi* (talcum) for Heat problems causing painful urination; with *zhi zi* (gardenia seeds) where urinary problems are associated with Damp Heat in the lower *jiao*; and with *dan shen* (Chinese sage) for some menstrual disorders. It is included in several patent remedies including *hua san* (powder of eight) to correct urinary disturbance.

⊗ Avoid in pregnancy or if there is Spleen or Kidney Deficiency.

Other substances to clear Dampness

- **Talcum** (*hua shi*): used to clear Heat from the Urinary Bladder; applied topically for Damp skin lesions.

- **Rush pith** (*deng xin cao*; *Juncus effusus*): used to clear Damp and Heat from the Heart channel.

- **Knotgrass** (*bian xu*; *Polygonum aviculare*): used for Damp Heat in the Urinary Bladder.

- **Plantain seed** (*che qian zi*; *Plantago asiatica*): used for clearing Damp Heat and for eye problems associated with Deficient Liver and Kidney and also to clear Lung Heat causing coughing.

- **Job's tear seeds** (*Yi yi ren*; *Coix lachryma-jobi*): used for various sorts of oedema and are also added to remedies for Deficient Spleen to clear Heat and expel Wind-Dampness.

- **Stephania** (*Fang ji*; *Stephania tetranda or Aristolochia fangchi*): differentiated as *han fang ji* and *guang fang ji* respectively, used to expel Wind Dampness. *Guang fang ji* is toxic and is to be avoided.

HERBS THAT EXPEL WIND DAMPNESS

These herbs clear Wind Dampness affecting the muscles, joints, bones, tendons and ligaments which cause 'Painful Obstruction' and *bi* syndrome – disorders which conventional medicine may label as arthritis, rheumatism, sciatica or gout, for example. Painful Obstruction disorders can be linked to Wind, Cold, Damp or Heat so herbs in this group can vary significantly in character. Many are also tonic remedies for Kidney or Liver associated in the five-element model with bones and tendons respectively.

Pubescent angelica root

Chinese name *Du huo*

Botanical name *Angelica pubescens*

Taste Pungent, bitter

Character Slightly warm

Meridians Kidney, Urinary Bladder

Actions Antirheumatic, analgesic, antiinflammatory, sedative, hypotensive, nervous stimulant

Du hou is specific for clearing Wind-Damp and relieving pain, especially Wind-Cold-Damp syndromes in the lower part of the body, and is used to combat attack by the external pathogens Wind and Damp so is helpful for superficial syndromes such as colds, rheumatic aches and pains, toothache and headaches.

Applications *Du hou* is one of the main ingredients in *du huo ji sheng tang* (decoction of pubescent angelica and mulberry mistletoe) and is used for arthritic pains and sciatica. It is used with *bo he* (field mint) and *fu ling* (tuckahoe) for external Wind-Cold-Damp disorders.

⊗ Avoid in *yin* Deficiency and Excess Fire syndromes.

Pubescent angelica root

Cocklebur fruit

Chinese name *Cang er zi*

Botanical name *Xanthium strumarium*

Taste Pungent, slightly bitter

Character Warm, slightly toxic

Meridians Lung, Liver

Actions Antibacterial, antifungal, antispasmodic, analgesic, antirheumatic

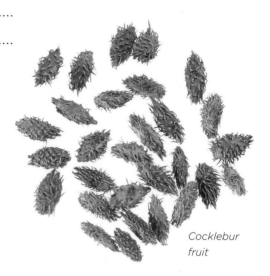

Cocklebur fruit

As well as clearing Wind-Damp, *cang er zi* is said to be helpful for catarrhal conditions such as allergic rhinitis and sinusitis. It also clears external Wind and is used when Wind-Damp causes itching.

Applications *Cang er zi* is combined with herbs such as *xin yi hua* (magnolia flowers), *shi gao* (gypsum) and *huang qin* (*baikal* skullcap) for acute Wind-Heat syndromes; with *wu wei zi* schizandra fruits) and *jin ying zi* (rosehips) for allergic rhinitis; and with *jin yin hua* (honeysuckle flowers) for chronic Wind-Heat disorders. With *huang qi* (astragalus root) and *bai zhu* (white atractylodes) it is used as a tonic remedy where *wei qi* is weak.

⊗ Avoid *cang er zi* in headache or Painful Obstruction caused by Deficient Blood.

Other herbs that expel Wind Dampness

- **Large-leaf gentian root** (*qin jiao*; *Gentiana macrophylla*): used for Wind-Damp Painful Obstruction and to moisten the Intestines in constipation.

- **Siberian ginseng root bark** (*qi jia pi*; *Eleutherococcus senticosus*): recommended for elderly people who have problems walking and to enhance stamina.

- **Mulberry twigs** *Sang zhi* (*Morus alba*): are used for Wind Dampness causing Painful Obstruction.

HERBS TO CLEAR PHLEGM AND STOP COUGHING

In Chinese medicine Phlegm is not just the sputum coughed up by the lung but a pathological accumulation of thick fluid that can affect other parts of the body especially the Channels, Stomach and Spleen. If Phlegm stagnates in the Channels it can cause goitre and lymphatic swellings; in the Stomach it can lead to nausea and vomiting, and in the Lungs to coughing and wheezing. Phlegm obstructing the Heart can cause strokes and seizures.

HERBS TO COOL AND TRANSFORM HOT PHLEGM

These herbs are cold and are used to treat coughs and swellings due to Hot Phlegm such as scrofula and goitre. Most are antitussive, expectorant, sedative and antiinflammatory.

Fritillary bulbs

Fritillary bulb

Chinese name *Zhe bei mu*

Botanical name *Fritillaria thunbergii*

Taste Bitter

Character Cold

Meridians Lung, Heart

Actions Antitussive, hypotensive, muscle relaxant

Zhe bei mu is used to clear and transform Hot Phlegm that can cause productive coughs. It also combats Heat and is used to reduce swellings including abscesses. Several species of Fritillaria are used in Chinese medicine — *chuan bei mu* (*F. cirrhosa*) is also used for cooling and transforming Hot Phlegm. Not as strong as *zhe bei mu*, it is more suitable for non-productive coughs. Both plants are sometimes used together simply as *bei mu*.

Applications *Zhe bei mu* is combined with *lian qi*ao (forsythia fruits) and *niu bang* zi (burdock seeds) for coughs with thick yellow sputum caused by Wind-Heat. With *xuan shen* (Ningpo figwort root) and *xia ku cao* (self-heal spikes), it is used for Phlegm Fire causing painful swellings and with *yi yi ren* (Job's tear seeds) and other herbs for lung abscesses.

⊗ Avoid *zhe bei mu* in Deficient Spleen patterns.

Other herbs to cool and transform Phlegm

- **Peucedanum root** (*qian hu*; *Peucedanum praeruptorum*): used to direct *qi* downwards as well as clear Phlegm. It is also used for pathogenic Wind conditions.

- **Snakegourd fruit** (*gua lou* (*Trichosanthes kirilowii*): is used to moisten the Lung, resolve Phlegm and also to invigorate Lung *qi*.

Peucedanum root

WARM HERBS TO TRANSFORM COLD PHLEGM

These herbs are warm and can be toxic so care is needed in both their preparation and in their use.

Pinellia tuber

Chinese name *Ban xia*

Botanical name *Pinellia ternata*

Taste Pungent

Character Warm, toxic

Meridians Lung, Spleen, Stomach

Actions Antiemetic, antitussive, expectorant, lowers blood cholesterol levels, antidote for strychnine poisoning

Ban xia is effective for drying Dampness and transforming Phlegm. It also reverses the flow of rebellious *qi*, responsible for certain types of vomiting and productive coughs. *Ban xia* clears Damp Phlegm from the Stomach, and dispels nodules and discomfort in the chest. It is usually soaked in tea or vinegar before use to reduce its toxicity.

Applications *Ban xia* is used in numerous remedies for Phlegm related disorders. With *gan jiang* (dried ginger) it subdues Rebellious *qi* caused by *yang* Deficiency and clears Cold; with *chen pi* (tangerine peel) and other herbs it is used for

productive coughs caused by Damp Phlegm Obstruction or Deficient Spleen *qi*.

⊗ Avoid in bleeding, Deficient *yin* coughs, pregnancy and Phlegm-Heat conditions. Long-term over-use can lead to loss of taste and numbness in the mouth and throat.

Pinellia tuber

Balloon flower root

Chinese name *Jie geng*

Botanical name *Platycodon grandiflorum*

Taste Pungent, bitter

Character Neutral

Meridians Lung

Actions Anti-fungal, anti-bacterial, expectorant, hypoglycemic, reduces cholesterol levels

Balloon flower root

Jie geng helps circulate Lung *qi* and clear Phlegm, especially when caused by Wind-Heat or Wind-Cold; it is also useful for sore throats and laryngitis associated with external Heat, Deficient *yin* with Heat signs and Hot Phlegm. It is one of the directional herbs focusing the remedy upwards to the upper part of the body.

Applications *Jie geng* is used with *gan cao* (liquorice) for swellings and pain in the throat caused by Wind-Heat and with *zi su ye* (perilla leaf) for productive coughs due to external Wind-Cold. It is combined with *ban xia* (pinellia) for coughs caused by Damp Phlegm.

⊗ Avoid in tuberculosis or if symptoms including the coughing up of blood.

Other warm herbs to transform Cold Phlegm

- **Japanese elecampane flower head** (*xuan fu hua*; *Inula brittanica*): also a directional remedy correcting the upward flow of Lung and Stomach *qi* that may cause coughs; it resolves Phlegm Stagnation in the Lung.

- **White mustard seed** (*bai jie zi*; *Brassica alba*): helps to warm Lung *qi* and ease pain caused by Cold Phlegm in the Channels. It is used for both pleurisy and joint pain.

HERBS TO RELIEVE COUGHING AND WHEEZING

These herbs provide symptomatic relief so are always combined with appropriate remedies to treat the underlying cause; they are generally antitussive, expectorant and antibiotic.

Bitter apricot seeds

Chinese name *Xing ren*

Botanical name *Prunus armeniaca*

Taste Bitter

Character Slightly warm, slightly toxic

Meridians Lung, Large Intestine

Actions Antitussive, antiasthmatic, antibacterial, antiparasitic, analgesic

Xing ren is used where symptoms include coughing caused by Cold or Heat problems. The seeds are effective for dry coughs and also to moisten the intestines in constipation. *Xing ren* is generally steamed or baked before use to reduce toxicity.

Applications *Xing ren* is used with herbs such as *huo ma ren* (hemp seed) for constipation caused by dryness or Deficient *qi* and with *shi gao* (gypsum), *zhe bei mu* (fritillary bulb) and *gua lou zi* (snakegourd fruit) for External Wind-Heat problems with cough producing thick, yellow sputum.

⊗ Avoid in coughs caused by Deficient yin. Apricot seeds contain hydrocyanic acid and high doses can be toxic.

Processed bitter apricot seeds

Mulberry root bark

Chinese name *sang bai pi*

Botanical name *Morus alba*

Taste Sweet

Character Cold

Meridians Lung, Spleen

Actions Various parts of the mulberry are analgesic, antiasthmatic, antibacterial, antitussive, diaphoretic, diuretic, expectorant, hypotensive, hypoglycemic, and sedative

Sliced mulberry root bark

Sang bai pi is largely used as a cough remedy for Heat in the Lung and asthma. Mulberry twigs (*sang zhi*) are used for rheumatic pains and spasms while the leaf (*sang ye*) is for Wind and Heat and the fruits (*sang shen*) nourish the Blood.

Applications *Sang bai pi* is also a diuretic and used with herbs such as *fu ling pi* (tuckahoe skin), and *chen pi* (tangerine peel) for oedema caused by Fluid imbalance associated with Deficient Spleen *qi*.

⊗ Avoid the root bark in Cold conditions and Deficient Lung.

Other herbs to relieve coughing and wheezing

- **Coltsfoot flower** (*kuan dong hua*; *Tussilago farfara*): redirects *qi* downwards and stops coughing.

- **Perilla seed** (*zi su zi*; *Perilla frutescens*): redirects *qi* downwards, dissolves Phlegm and also moistens the Intestines in constipation caused by Dryness.

- **Purple aster root** (*zi wan*; *Aster tartaricus*): stops a wide range of coughs epecially where Cold and copious sputum are involved.

AROMATIC HERBS

These herbs are used to clear Dampness associated with Stagnation of the middle *jiao* with nausea, vomiting, abdominal distention and loss of appetite. They are all pungent and dry and must be used with some caution if there is any *yin* Deficiency.

Patchouli or giant hyssop

Chinese name *Huo xiang*

Botanical names *Pogostemon cablin* or *Agastache rugosa*

Taste Pungent

Character Slightly warm

Meridians Lung, Spleen, Stomach

Actions Antibacterial, antifungal, diaphoretic, digestive tonic

Huo xiang can be two different plants. Both patchouli (*Pogostemon cablin*) and giant hyssop (*Agastache rugosa*) are used medicinally as *huo xiang*. As well as clearing Damp it dispels Cold and harmonizes the middle *jiao*.

Applications *Hou xiang* is included in *huo xiang zheng qi san* (powder for dispelling turbidity with giant hyssop), which is used to clear Dampness from Spleen and Stomach. For acute diarrhoea associated with Heat and Dampness, it is used with such herbs as *huang qin baikal* (skullcap) and *lian qiao* (forsythia fruits).

⊗ Avoid in fevers and Interior Heat syndromes.

Giant hyssop flower head

Grey atractylodes rhizome

Chinese name *Cang zhu*

Botanical name *Atractylodes chinensis*

Taste Pungent, bitter

Character Warm

Meridians Spleen, Stomach

Actions Carminative, diaphoretic, increases excretion of sodium and potassium salts, although it is not diuretic

Cang zhu is used for Dampness in the lower *jiao*, Wind-Dampness associated with painful obstruction, Dampness causing Spleen problems and also for external problems associated with Wind-Cold-Damp.

Applications *Cang zhu* is used for digestive problems associated with Damp Cold stagnating in the Spleen with herbs such as *hou po* (magnolia bark) and *chen pi* (tangerine peel). *Cang zhu* is a traditional remedy for night blindness and cataracts when combined with *hei zhi ma* (sesame seeds) and other herbs.

⊗ Avoid in *qi* or *yin* Deficiency associated with Interior Heat.

Other aromatic herbs to transform Dampness

- **Magnolia bark** (*huo po*; *Magnolia officinalis*): used to move *qi*, warm and transform Phlegm, and clear Stagnation. It is used for both digestive and respiratory problems.

- **Grains of paradise or bastard cardamomis** (*sha ren*; *Amomum xanthoides*): are used to move *qi*, strengthen the Stomach and calm the foetus in morning sickness.

AROMATIC HERBS TO OPEN ORIFICES

These are mainly used for 'Locked-in Syndrome' (*bì zhèng*) following strokes that lead to coma and rigid limbs. They stimulate the central nervous system and can drain congenital *qi* so should only be used for a short time.

- **Borneol resin** (*bing pian*; *Dryobalanops aromatica*): used for fainting and convulsions

- **Sweetflag rhizome** (*shi chang pu*, also called *chang pu*; *Acorus gramineus*): clears Phlegm that causes deafness, dizziness and dulled senses.

HERBS TO RELIEVE FOOD STAGNATION

Symptoms of food stagnation include abdominal distention and nausea with a preference for either hot or cold foods depending on whether the stagnation is a Cold disorder or a Hot one. The herbs in this group are mainly digestive stimulants.

Radish seed

Chinese name *Lai fu zi*

Botanical name *Raphanus sativa*

Taste Pungent, sweet

Character Neutral

Meridians Lung, Spleen, Stomach

Actions Antimicrobial, antifungal

As well as dissolving Food Stagnation, *lai fu zi* causes *qi* to descend and transforms Phlegm so is also used in chronic coughs.

Radish seeds

Applications *Lai fu zi* is combined with *shan zha* (hawthorn berries) or *chen pi* (tangerine peel) for Food Stagnation; and is used with *ban xia* (pinellia), *xing ren* (bitter apricot seeds) or *zi su zi* (perilla seeds) where there is coughing associated with Damp Phlegm or excess Heat.

⊗ Use *lai fu zi* cautiously if there is Deficient *yin*.

Chinese hawthorn berries

Chinese hawthorn berries

Chinese name *Shan zha*

Botanical name *Crataegus pinnatifida*

Taste Sour, sweet

Character Slightly warm

Meridians Spleen, Stomach, Liver

Actions Antibacterial, hypotensive, peripheral vasodilator, cardiac tonic, lowers cholesterol levels

As well as easing food stagnation, *shan zha* is used to invigorate Blood circulation and generally improve digestive processes.

Applications *Shan zha* is traditionally combined with *mai ya* (barley sprouts) and *shen qu* (medicated leaves) for food stagnation. *Shan zha* is also used with remedies like *dang gui* (Chinese angelica) for Congealed Blood that can cause some menstrual pain.

⊗ Avoid or use *shan zha* cautiously in cases of Deficient Spleen and Stomach and if there is acid regurgitation.

Barley sprouts

Chinese name *Mai ya*

Botanical name *Hordium vulgare*

Taste Sweet

Character Slightly warm

Meridians Spleen, Stomach

Actions Contains enzymes and vitamin B, which aid digestion

While barley sprouts are used in decoctions and powders with other herbs, they are also eaten either raw or toasted to clear Food Stagnation or strengthen the Spleen. They also reduce milk flow and are traditionally taken for weaning, when they should be stir fried. *Mai ya* can also be given to babies to treat milk regurgitation and dyspepsia in babies.

Applications *Mai ya* is combined with a number of herbs including *fu ling* (tuckahoe) and *bai zhu* (white atractylodes) in *jian pi wan* (strengthening the Spleen pills) used for Spleen and Stomach Deficiency with Food Stagnation. It is used with *gan jiang* (dried ginger) for indigestion associated with Stomach Deficiency.

⊗ Avoid when breast feeding.

HERBS TO WARM THE INTERIOR AND EXPEL COLD

Interior Cold can be caused by pathogenic Cold invading the body or by internally generated Cold, sometimes associated with shock or Deficiency syndromes. Herbs to expel Cold generally warm the Spleen and Kidney and are often used with herbs that tonify *yang* or *qi*.

Cloves

Chinese name *Ding xiang*

Botanical name *Syzygium aromaticum*

Taste Pungent

Character Warm

Meridians Spleen, Stomach, Kidney

Actions Carminative, antiemetic, antibacterial, analgesic, antiinflammatory, causes uterine contractions

Cloves are used in Chinese medicine to warm the *san jiao* and Kidneys and also to cause Rebellious *qi* to descend. The herb also strengthens Kidney.

Applications Cloves are used with *wu zhu yu* (evodia berries) for abdominal pain and vomiting associated with Cold Stomach and with *rou gui* (cinnamon bark) for impotence associated with deficient Kidneys.

⊗ Avoid in *yin* Deficiency and Heat syndromes.

Cloves

Evodia berries

Chinese name *Wu zhu yu*

Botanical name *Evodia rutacarpa*

Taste Pungent, bitter

Character Hot, slightly toxic

Meridians Spleen, Stomach, Liver, Kidney

Actions Antibacterial, antiparasitic, analgesic, raises body temperature, respiratory stimulant, uterine stimulant

Wu zhu yu warms the Spleen and Stomach and also reverses the flow of *qi* associated with vomiting and acid regurgitation.

Applications *Wu zhu yu* is traditionally mixed with liquorice water to reduce its toxicity or cooked with ginger to relieve abdominal pain caused by Cold. When stir-baked (stir-fried without oil) it is used to reverse the upward flow of Stomach and Liver *qi*.

⊗ Avoid *wu zhu yu* in *yin* Deficiency and Excess Fire.

Other herbs to warm the interior and expel cold

- **Dry Ginger** (*Gan jiang*; *Zingiber officinale*): has a tonic action and enters the Kidney meridian, where it is used to replenish *yang*, expel Cold and warm Spleen and Stomach.

- **Cinnamon bark** (*Rou gui*; *Cinnamomum cassia*): as well as clearing Interior Cold, is used to warm and tonify the Kidneys.

- **Fennel seeds** (*xiao hui xiang*; *Foeniculum vulgare*): regulate *qi* and warm the *san jiao*; as in the West they are mainly used for digestive problems.

- **Galangal rhizome** (*Gao liang jiang*; *Alpinia officinarum*): used to warm the middle *jiao* and relieve pain.

Galangal

HERBS TO REGULATE QI

These herbs can be divided into two groups — herbs to move Stagnant *qi* and tonic herbs used in Deficient *qi* disorders.

HERBS TO MOVE STAGNANT QI

Stagnant *qi* conditions are characterized by pain in the organs affected. These herbs tend to be dry so prolonged use can damage *yin*.

Tangerine peel

Chinese name *Chen pi*

Botanical name *Citrus reticulata*

Taste Pungent, bitter

Character Warm

Meridians Lung, Spleen, Stomach

Actions Anti-asthmatic, anti-inflammatory, carminative, digestive stimulant, expectorant, circulatory stimulant; trials have shown it to be effective for acute mastitis

Chen pi is the ripe peel from tangerines or mandarins while *qing pi* is the green peel from the same unripe fruit and enters Liver and Gall Bladder meridians.

Applications *Chen pi* is a widely used ingredient in remedies for coughing and nausea where disordered *qi* is to blame. For problems associated with Stagnant Spleen and Stomach *qi*, it is used in *ping wei san* (calm Stomach powder). *Chen pi* improves with storage.

⊗ Avoid in cases of coughing up blood or if there is no sign of Damp/ Phlegm stagnation.

Shredded tangerine peel

Nutgrass tuber

Chinese name *Xiang fu*

Botanical name *Cyperus rotundus*

Taste Pungent, slightly bitter

Character Neutral

Meridians Liver, Stomach

Actions Analgesic, antibacterial, antispasmodic for the uterus

Nutgrass tuber

Xiang fu helps to circulate *qi* especially where Constrained Liver *qi* is the problem, and is used for menstrual problems normalizing the cycle and easing period pains. It is prepared with vinegar to enhance its painkilling effect or salt to help moisten Blood and Fluids.

Applications *Xiang fu* is used with *bai zhu* (white atractylodes) and *ban xia* (pinellia) for Spleen or Stomach Deficiency and added to mixtures like *xiang sha ping wei san* (nutgrass and grains of paradise powder to calm the Stomach). It is used with *dang gui* (Chinese angelica) for menstrual irregularities.

⊗ Avoid in Heat syndromes associated with *yin* Deficiency.

Other herbs to move Stagnant qi

- **Costus root** (*mu xiang*; *Saussurea kappa* or *Vladimiria souliei*): mainly used for problems with Spleen or Stomach *qi*.

- **Sandalwood** (*tan xiang*; *Santalum album*): used for Stagnant Spleen or Stomach *qi*.

- **Bitter (Seville) orange** (*zhi shi* and *zhi ke*; *Citrus aurantium*): immature fruit used to break up Stagnant *qi* and direct it downwards.

- **Chinese chive** (*xie bai*; *Allium macrostemon*): used to move *qi* and Blood and also dissipate Cold Phlegm; it directs *qi* downwards.

- **Betel husk** (*da fu pi*; *Areca catechu*): used for Spleen and Stomach *qi* Stagnation.

HERBS TO TONIFY QI

These herbs are used in *qi* Deficiency where particular organs or functions are weak — most commonly Lungs or Spleen. They are sweet and rich and over-use can lead to sensations of heat or fullness in the upper body. It is best to avoid taking tonic herbs when suffering from infectious diseases.

Korean ginseng root

Chinese name *Ren shen*

Botanical name *Panax ginseng*

Taste Sweet, slightly bitter

Character Warm

Meridians Spleen, Lung, Heart

Actions Tonic, stimulant, reduces blood sugar and cholesterol levels, immunostimulant

Korean or red ginseng is the best known of China's many tonic herbs. It is used to replenish and tonify *qi*, to generate body fluids and to combat fatigue.

Applications *Ren shen* is a powerful *qi* tonic and is included in many formulae. With *bai zhu* (white atractylodes) it is used for Deficient Spleen and Stomach *qi*; with *fu ling* (tuckahoe) for Deficient Heart and Spleen; or with *wu wei zi* (schizandra) for Deficient *qi* and *yin* conditions.

⊗ Avoid in Heat conditions.

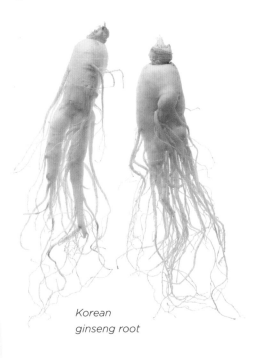

Korean ginseng root

Milk vetch root

Chinese name *Huang qi*

Botanical name *Astragalus membranaceus*

Taste Sweet

Character Slightly warm

Meridians Spleen, Lung

Actions Antispasmodic, diuretic, cholagogue, antibacterial, hypoglycemic, nervous stimulant, hypotensive, immune stimulant

Huang qi helps to strengthen defence energy, so is believed to boost the immune system. It also encourages wound healing and helps regulate water metabolism, as well as tonifying *qi* and Blood.

Applications *Huang qi* is included with *ren shen* (Korean ginseng) and *bai zhu* (white atractylodes) in *bu zhong yi qi tang* used to combat Spleen and Stomach Deficiency or with *dang gui* (Chinese angelica) to nourish blood in anaemia and Blood Deficiency.

• Avoid in Excess syndromes or if there is Deficient *yin*.

White atractylodes rhizome

Chinese name *Bai zhu*

Botanical name *Atractylodes macrocephala*

Taste Sweet, bitter

Character Warm

Meridians Spleen, Stomach

Actions Antibacterial, anticoagulant, digestive stimulant, diuretic, hypoglycemic

Bai zhu tonifies the Spleen and dispels Dampness so tends to be used where symptoms include poor appetite, indigestion, chronic diarrhoea and abdominal fullness. It can also help to boost the *wei qi* to increase resistance in Exterior syndromes.

Applications *Bai zhu* is included in the famous energy-giving *si jun zi tang* (four noble ingredients decoction) with *ren shen* (Korean ginseng), *fu ling* (tuckahoe), and *gan cao* (liquorice).

⊗ Avoid in *yin* Deficiency characterized by extreme thirst.

Chinese dates

Chinese name *Da zao* and *hong zao*

Botanical name *Zizi phus vulgaris var. jujuba*

Taste Sweet

Character Warm

Meridians Spleen, Stomach

Actions Nutrient, protects against liver damage

Chinese red dates

Da zao and *hong zao* are from the same kind of fruit — when blanched slightly in boiling water and dried under the sun, it is *hong zao* (red *jujube*), and when the fruit is blanched in boiling water and baked until the skin become black and shiny it is called *da zao* (large *jujube*). Both nourish the Blood (*hong zao* rather more effectively) and calm the Spirit.

Applications *Da zao* is often combined with harsh cathartic herbs to modify their action and prevent injury to Stomach and Spleen. Chinese dates also 'calm the Spirit' so are used for symptoms associated with Deficient Heart syndromes.

⊗ Avoid in cases of Excess Dampness, Food Stagnation or Phlegm.

Liquorice root

Chinese name *Gan cao*

Botanical name *Glycyrrhiza uralensis*

Taste Sweet

Character Neutral (raw) or warm (prepared)

Meridians Heart, Lung, Spleen, Stomach

Actions Antibacterial, antitussive, antiinflammatory, antispasmodic, antiallergenic, hypotensive, steroidal action, cholagogue

Liquorice root

Gan cao is used to invigorate *qi*, tonify the Spleen, moisten the Lungs to stop coughing and wheezing, and also to clear Heat and Fire Poisons. It is often added to prescriptions to harmonize the action of other herbs.

Applications *Gan cao* is used with *dang shen* (bellflower root) for Deficient Spleen with *gui zhi* (cinnamon twigs) added where there is deficient Heart *qi*. It is used with *bai shao yao* (white peony) for Liver Blood problems associated with pain in the abdomen or with *chen pi* (tangerine peel) and *ban xia* (pinellia) in *er chen tang* (decoction of two old herbs) used to transform and clear Phlegm in chronic bronchitis.

⊗ Avoid in excess Dampness, nausea or vomiting.

Other herbs to tonify qi

- **Bellflower root** (*dang shen*; *Codonopsis pilosula*): an important tonic that is more *yin* in character than *ren shen* (Korean ginseng) and is traditionally taken by nursing mothers. It is included in *ba zhen tang* (eight treasures decoction) for Deficient *qi* and Blood.

- **Chinese yam root** (*shan yao*; *Dioscorea opposita*): used to tonify *qi* of Spleen and Stomach but also nourishes Lung and Kidney.

HERBS TO REGULATE THE BLOOD

Herbs to regulate Blood come into three general categories: those to stop bleeding; those to invigorate the Blood (used in cases of Stagnant or Congealed Blood); and those that tonify the Blood (used when Blood is Deficient).

HERBS TO STOP BLEEDING

Used for a range of conditions ranging from nosebleeds and coughing up blood-streaked sputum to heavy menstrual periods and blood in the urine. They are generally combined with herbs that are appropriate for the underlying condition.

Notoginseng or pseudoginseng root

Chinese name *San qi*

Botanical name *Panax pseudoginseng*

Taste Sweet, slightly bitter

Character Warm

Meridians Liver, Stomach

Actions Antibacterial, antiinflammatory, cardiotonic, circulatory, stimulant, diuretic, haemostatic, hypoglycemic, peripheral vasodilator

San qi is used for bleeding associated with Congealed Blood — internally and externally — and will also reduce swelling and relieve pain so is often used for traumatic injuries. It helps to encourage Blood circulation so is also used for chest and abdominal pain.

Applications *San qi* is used by itself in *yun nan bai yao* (Yunnan white remedy) for a wide range of bleeding disorders. It is used in patent remedies such as *san qi shang yao pian* (notoginseng and peony pills), to ease pain in sprains and tendon injuries.

⊗ Avoid *san qi* in pregnancy and only use with caution in Deficient Blood syndromes.

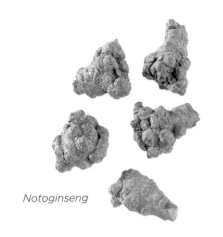

Notoginseng

Artemisia vulgaris
var. indica

Other herbs to stop bleeding

- **Bullrush pollen** (*pu huang*; *Typha latifolia* and other species): used to stop bleeding from external traumatic injuries as well as encouraging Blood circulation and dispelling Congealed Blood.

- **Mugwort leaf** (*ai ye*; *Artemisia vulgaris var. indica*): used in moxibustion but also warms the meridians and stops bleeding. It is included in *jiao ai tang* (donkey hide and mugwort decoction) which is a popular remedy to calm the foetus in threatened miscarriage.

- **Bletilla rhizome** (*bai ji*; *Bletilla striata*): used for bleeding from the Lungs and Stomach and also reduces swellings and encourages healing.

- **Arborvitae twigs** (*ce bai ye*; *Biota orientalis*): cool the Blood and relieve coughs; they are used for many bleeding disorders including bleeding gums and bleeding of the uterus.

HERBS TO INVIGORATE THE BLOOD

These herbs are used for problems associated with Stagnant or Congealed Blood that may cause pain, abscesses or ulcers, or Abdominal Swellings, such as tumours (*zheng jia*) and cysts.

Chinese sage root

Chinese name *Dan shen*

Botanical name *Salvia miltiorrhiza*

Taste Bitter

Character Slightly cold

Meridians Heart, Liver, Pericardium

Actions Anticoagulant, antibacterial, immune stimulant, circulatory stimulant, peripheral vasodilator, promotes tissue repair, sedative, lowers blood cholesterol, hypoglycemic

Chinese sage root

Dan shen clears Heat and 'calms the Spirit'. Modern studies have shown it to be effective for angina pectoris and problems associated with cerebral circulation.

Applications *Dan shen* is used with *dang gui* (Chinese angelica) for menstrual problems or with *mu dan pi* (tree peony bark) and *sheng di huang* (Chinese foxglove) for Warm-Febrile diseases.

⊗ Avoid if there is no Blood Stagnation.

Red peony root

Red peony root

Chinese name *Chi shao yao*

Botanical name *Paeonia lactiflora*

Taste Sour, bitter

Character Slightly cold

Meridians Liver, Spleen

Actions Antibacterial, anticoagulant, antiinflammatory, immune stimulant, lowers blood cholesterol, peripheral vasodilator, hypoglycemic, sedative, stimulates tissue repair, improves microcirculation

Red peony is used to clear Blood Stagnation, especially where symptoms include period pain, menstrual irregularities or Abdominal Swellings. It is also cooling for Heat in the Blood, especially in fevers and skin conditions, and clears Liver Fire.

Applications *Chi shao yao* is used with *ju hua* (chrysanthemum flowers) and *huang qin baikal* (skullcap) and other herbs for red, swollen eyes, or with *xiang fu* (nutgrass tuber) for period pain or Abdominal Swellings.

⊗ Avoid if there is no evidence of Blood Stagnation.

Other substances to invigorate the Blood

- **Ox knee root** (*huai nu xi*; *Achyranthis bidentata*): used to clear Damp Heat in the lower *jiao* and to descend the flow of Blood when caused by Deficient *yin* with ascending Fire.

- **Szechuan lovage root** (*chuan xiong*; *Ligusticum wallichii*): expels Wind, moves *qi* upwards, relieves pain, dizziness and headaches.

- **Corydalis rhizome** (*yan hu suo*; *Corydalis yanhusuo*): used for pain caused by Congealed Blood such as period pain; it also moves *qi*.

- **Peach seed** (*tao ren*; *Prunus persica*): used to break up Congealed Blood mainly in menstrual and abdominal problems and to moisten the intestines.

- **Safflower** (*hong hua*; *Carthamis tinctorius*): used for Congealed Blood in gynecological disorders.

- **Myrrh** (*mo yao*; *Commiphora myrrha*): also dispels Congealed Blood and promotes healing.

HERBS TO TONIFY THE BLOOD

These herbs are used for Deficient Blood syndromes and are said to 'nourish the Blood'. Typical symptoms include pale face and lips, dizziness, palpitations, dry skin and lethargy, associated with iron-deficient anaemia.

Fleeceflower root

Chinese name *He shou wu*

Botanical name *Polygonum multiflorum*

Taste Sweet, bitter, astringent

Character Slightly warm

Meridians Liver, Kidney

Actions Antibacterial, cardiotonic, hormonal action, hyperglycemic, laxative, liver stimulant, reduces blood cholesterol

Fleeceflower root

He shou wu is specific for strengthening Kidney essence so is a valuable menopausal remedy. It is also a moist laxative, detoxifies Fire Poisons causing carbuncles and boils, and expels External Wind by nourishing the Blood.

Applications *He shou wu* is combined with *xuan shen* (figwort root) and *lian qi*ao (forsythia fruits) for abscesses or with *gou qi zi* (wolfberry fruit) and *bu gu zi* (scuffy pea) for symptoms of premature ageing associated with deficient Liver and Kidney.

⊗ Avoid in diarrhoea associated with Phlegm or Deficient Spleen.

Chinese angelica root

Chinese name *Dang gui*

Botanical name *Angelica polyphorma var. sinensis*

Taste Sweet, pungent

Character Warm

Meridians Liver, Heart, Spleen

Actions Antibacterial, analgesic, antiinflammatory, circulatory stimulant, reduces blood cholesterol levels, liver tonic, sedative, uterine stimulant, rich in folic acid and vitamin B12

Sliced Chinese angelica root

Dang gui is also sold as *tang kwai* or *dong qui* in tinctures, tablets and powders, and is used to nourish and invigorate the Blood as well as ease pain from Congealed or Stagnant Blood. It is also a moist laxative used for constipation in the elderly.

Applications *Dang gui* is sometimes combined with *huang qi* (milk vetch root) for debility and fatigue associated with Deficient Blood or with *sheng jiang* (fresh ginger) for pain after childbirth. It is included in numerous classic formulae including *dang gui si ni tang* (Chinese angelica decoction for frigid extremities) also containing *gui zhi* (cinnamon twigs) and *bai shao yao* (white peony), used to disperse Cold and nourish Blood.

⊗ Avoid in pregnancy, diarrhoea or abdominal fullness.

White peony root

Chinese name *Bai shao yao*

Botanical name *Paeonia lactiflora*

Taste Sour, bitter

Character Slightly cold

Meridians Liver, Spleen

Actions Antibacterial, antiinflammatory, antispasmodic, diuretic, sedative, hypotensive, analgesic

Bai shao yao is used to nourish the Blood in Deficient Blood syndromes, it also calms the Liver and relieves pain associated with Constrained Liver *qi* or disharmony between Liver and Spleen. It is also used for Deficient *yin* problems and some Wind Cold syndromes.

Applications *Bai shao yao* is used with *chai hu* (thorowax root) and *zhi shi* (bitter orange) to calm Liver *qi* and regulate the Spleen; or with *gui zhi* (cinnamon twigs), *sheng jiang* (fresh ginger) and other herbs in *xiao jian zhong tang* (minor decoction to restore the middle *jiao*) for abdominal pain associated with *san jiao* weakness. With *gan cao* (liquorice) it is used to nourish the Liver and ease muscle cramps associated with Deficient Blood.

⊗ Avoid in diarrhoea and abdominal coldness.

White peony root

Wolfberry fruits

Chinese name *Gou qi shi*

Botanical name *Lycium barbarum or L. chinense*

Taste Sweet

Character Neutral

Meridians Liver, Kidney

Actions Hypotensive, hypoglycemic, immune stimulant, liver tonic and restorative, lowers blood cholesterol levels

Wolfberry fruits

Wolfberry fruits are used to nourish and tonify Liver and Kidney, and said to 'brighten the eyes', where Deficient Liver and Kidney is associated with blurred vision, dizziness and eyesight problems. In recent *years* the berries have gained in popularity as a health food under the name of goji berries.

Applications *Gou qi* zi is used with *shu di huang* (prepared Chinese foxglove) and other herbs for dizziness, tinnitus, impotence and weakness associated with Deficient *yin* and Blood or with *ju hua* (chrysanthemum flowers) where Deficiency symptoms include tinnitus, headache and eyesight problems.

⊗ Avoid in cases of Excess Heat, and Spleen Deficiency with Dampness.

Other herbs to tonify the Blood

- **Prepared Chinese foxglove root** (*shu di huang*; *Rehmannia glutinosa*): is the most widely used herb in this group, is slightly warm and as well as nourishing Blood, regulates menstrual flow and replenishes the vital essence of the Kidney.

- **Longan fruit flesh** (*long yan rou* also called *guiyuan rou*; *Dimocarpus longan*): used to tonify Heart and Spleen, nourish Blood and calm the Spirit and used for insomnia, palpitations and dizziness.

- **Mulberry fruits** (*sang shen*; *Morus alba*): nourish Blood and Liver and Kidney *yin*; also used for dizziness, insomnia and premature greying of the hair.

ASTRINGENT HERBS

These are used for treating conditions involving some sort of Excess discharge – such as diarrhoea, excess sweating, frequent urination or prolapse of the womb or rectum. All these herbs contain large amounts of tannin, which may explain their action.

Dogwood fruits

Chinese name *Shan zhu yu*

Botanical name *Cornus officinalis*

Taste Sour

Character Warm

Meridians Liver, Kidney

Actions Antibacterial, antifungal, diuretic, hypotensive, styptic

Dogwood fruits

Shan zhu yu stops bleeding so is often used for excessive menstrual bleeding. It helps replenish Liver and Kidney essence so is helpful where symptoms include aching back and knees, vertigo, frequent urination and sweating.

Applications *Shan zhu yu* is combined with *shu di huang* (prepared Chinese foxglove) and *fu ling* (tuckahoe) in *liu wei di huang wan* (six ingredients Chinese foxglove pill) used to nourish Liver and Kidney *yin*. With *huang qi* (milk vetch) and *dang shen* (bellflower root) it is used for spontaneous sweating associated with *yang* or *qi* Deficiency and with *bai shao yao* (white peony) for excessive uterine bleeding.

⊗ Avoid *shan zhu yu* in Fire symptoms and Deficiency Kidney *yang*; it should not be combined with *jie geng* (balloon flower root) or *fang feng* (siler).

Schizandra fruits

Chinese name *Wu wei zi*

Botanical name *Schisandra chinensis*

Taste Sour

Character Warm

Meridians Lung, Heart, Kidney

Actions Antibacterial, astringent, aphrodisiac, circulatory stimulant, digestive stimulant, expectorant, hypotensive, sedative, tonic

Wu wei zi is used to replenish *qi*, especially Lung *qi*, tonify the Kidney and Heart, calm the Spirit, and control excessive sweating. It is used for a condition sometimes called 'cock-crow diarrhoea'.

Applications *Wu wei zi* is included in many patent remedies. It is used with *ren shen* (Korean ginseng) and *mai men dong* (lily turf root) to control sweating and tonify *qi* or with warming herbs including *gan jiang* (dry ginger) and *gui zhi* (cinnamon twigs) to disperse Cold and warm the Lungs in asthma and chills.

⊗ Avoid in cases of Internal Heat and superficial syndromes.

Other astringent herbs

- **Cherokee rosehips** (*jin ying zi*; *Rosa laevigata*): used for Kidney *jing* problems and diarrhoea.

- **Natgalls** (*wu bei zi*; *Rhus chinensis*): used to combat leakage of Lung *qi* causing Deficient Lung; and from the intestines causing diarrhoea.

- **Rou dou kou** (Myristica fragrans): nutmeg is used to warm the middle *jiao* and control diarrhoea.

- **Praying mantis egg cases** (*sang piao xiao*; *Paratendera sinensis*): mainly used in Deficient Kidney *yang* syndromes.

- **Ailanthus root** (*chun pi*; *Ailanthus altissima*): used to clear Heat and Damp causing diarrhoea or vaginal discharge.

- **Black plum** (*wu mei*; *Prunus mume*): used to combat leakage in coughing and diarrhoea, and to stop bleeding. It is used topically for corns and warts.

HERBS TO TONIFY YANG

Tonic herbs – including those for the Blood and *qi* are used to treat Deficiency syndromes and help to strengthen processes in the body. This can include Exterior conditions, and tonics should always be used with caution in *ling*ering superficial syndromes as they can worsen rather than improve the condition. Herbs to tonify *yang* are most often needed for Deficient Kidney *yang* since the Kidney stores Congenital *qi* which is the basis of the body's *yang*. Symptoms can include exhaustion, cold extremities, 'cock-crow diarrhoea', wheezing and excessive urination.

Caterpillar fungus

Chinese name *Dong chong xia cao*

Botanical name *Cordyceps sinensis*

Taste Sweet

Character Neutral

Meridians Lung, Kidney

Actions Stimulates adrenal glands, antibacterial, sedative, hypnotic, some anticancer activity

Dong chong xia cao is a fungus that grows on the noses of certain types of caterpillars. Modern supplies are grown on grain so the caterpillar is no longer essential. The fungus replenishes Lung and Kidney *yang* and also nourishes *yin* making it a balanced remedy for long-term use.

Applications *Dong chong xia cao* is used to boost *yang* energies and *wei qi*. It is used with *xing ren* (bitter apricot) and *chuan bei mu* (fritillary) for Deficient Lung *yin*. Today it is available in powdered form, often mixed with other medicinal fungi, which can be stirred into yoghurt or fruit juice.

⊗ Avoid if there are external pathogenic symptoms.

Caterpillar fungus

Other substances to tonify yang

- **Scuffy pea seed** (*bu gu zhi*; *Psoralea corylifolia*): used to tonify Kidney and Spleen *yang* and treat cock-crow diarrhoea.

- **Walnuts** (*hu tao ren*; *Juglans regia*): a Kidney *yang* tonic that also nourishes the Lung and act as a moist laxative.

- **Morinda root** (*ba ji tian*; *Morinda officinalis*): used to tonify Kidney *yang* and disperse Wind and Cold-Damp.

- **Goatwort** (*yin yang huo*, or *xian ling pi*; *Epimedium grandiflorum*): used for Deficient Kidney *yang* and to expel Wind-Cold Dampness.

- **Golden eye-grass rhizome** (*xian mao*; *Curculigo orchioides*): tonifies Kidney *yang* and is used for infertility problems; it also expels Cold and Damp.

- **Fenugreek seeds** (*hu lu ba*; *Trigonella foenum-graecum*): used for Deficient Kidney *yang* associated with Cold and *qi* Stagnation.

- **Dodder seeds** (*tu si zi*; *Cuscuta chinensis*): used to tonify the Kidneys in Deficient Kidney *yang* syndromes and also calm the foetus in threatened miscarriage.

- **Eucommia bark** (*du zhong*; *Eucommia ulmoides*): is used for Liver and Kidney *yang* Deficiency and to encourage the smooth flow of *qi* and Blood.

HERBS TO TONIFY YIN

These herbs tonify *yin* of Lung, Stomach, Kidney or Liver and are generally nourishing and moistening. They are combined with other herbs for conditions involving Dryness, Phlegm or a lack of Body Fluids where symptoms include constipation, dry mouth, thirst and feverish conditions.

False daisy

Chinese name *Han lian cao*

Botanical name *Eclipta prostrata*

Taste Sweet, sour

Character Cold

Meridians Liver, Kidney

Actions Antibacterial, hemostatic

Han lian cao is generally used for conditions that involve tinnitus, premature greying of head hair, teeth problems and bleeding. In Chinese folk tradition it is used for skin problems such as athlete's foot and dermatitis.

Applications *Han lian cao* is combined with *nu zhen zi* (glossy privet berries) for dizziness and premature greying of the hair associated with Kidney Deficiency; with various herbs for different sorts of bleeding, with *ai ye* (mugwort), for example, it is used for uterine bleeding associated with Deficient *yin* syndromes.

⊗ Avoid in Cold and Deficiency syndromes of Spleen and Kidney.

False daisy

Privet berries

Glossy privet berries

Chinese name *Nu zhen zi*

Botanical name *Ligustrum lucidum*

Taste Sweet, bitter

Character Neutral

Meridians Liver, Kidney

Actions Antibacterial, cardiotonic, diuretic, immune stimulant

Nu zhen zi nourishes and tonifies the vital essence of Liver and Kidney. Like other Kidney *yin* herbs it helps to restore colour to greying hair and also strengthens the knees and waist.

Applications *Nu zhen zi* is included in various formulae – with *bu gu zhi* (scuffy pea seeds) it is used for dizziness and lower back weakness associated with Deficient Kidney *yin*.

⊗ Avoid in diarrhoea with Deficiency of *yang*.

Other herbs to tonify yin

- **Black sesame seeds** (*hei zhi ma* or *hu ma ren*; *Sesamum indicum*): used to nourish Liver and Kidney *yin*, Blood and moisten the Intestines in constipation.

- **Lily-turf root** (*mai men dong*; *Ophiopogon japonicus* or *Liriope minor*): used to moisten the Lung to ease dry coughs and in Heat conditions where *yin* is diminished.

- **American ginseng root** (*xi yang shen*; *Panax quinquifolius*): used for chronic dry coughs associated with Lung *yin* Deficiency.

- **Orchid stems** (*shi hu*; *Dendrobium nobile*): good for Deficient Stomach *yin* and to strengthen Kidney *yin*.

- **Solomon's seal root** (*yu zhu*; *Polygonatum odoratum*): specific for nourishing Lung and Stomach yin, it is used for dizziness associated with Deficient *yin* and Wind.

- **Mulberry mistletoe** (*sang ji sheng*; *Loranthus parasiticus* or *Viscum coloratum*): both are used to tonify Liver and Kidney yin, expel Wind-Dampness and nourish Blood.

SUBSTANCES TO CALM THE SPIRIT

This category includes many non-herbs such as shells and minerals to calm disturbances of Heart *shen* (Spirit) that can lead to irritability, insomnia and mental disorders. They are divided into two groups: substances to settle the Spirit; and substances that nourish the Heart.

SUBSTANCES TO SETTLE AND CALM THE SPIRIT

Shells and minerals are seen as heavy and solid so weigh upon the Heart and prevent the fluttering of the Spirit which may manifest as palpitations and insomnia. They also weigh down over-exuberant Liver *yang* and redirect Rebellious *qi* downwards.

Mother-of-pearl

Chinese name *Zhen shu mu*

Zoological name *Pteria margaritifera*

Taste Sweet, salty

Character Cold

Meridians Heart, Liver

Actions Little known

As well as settling the spirit, *zhen zhu* mu controls over-exuberant Liver *yang* that can cause eye problems and blurred vision. It is said to help when 'Heart and Spirit are not at peace' leading to easy anger, fright and insomnia.

Applications Mother-of-pearl is used with herbs *dang gui* (Chinese angelica) and *shu di huang* (prepared Chinese foxglove) to calm the Heart and mind and nourish *yin* and Blood. It is used with other minerals and shells for palpitations, anxiety and seizures or with substances such as *bing pian* (borneol) in topical treatments for sore eyes or ulceration.

⊗ Avoid if there is abdominal Cold.

HERBS THAT NOURISH THE HEART AND CALM THE SPIRIT

These remedies are mainly used for Deficient Heart Blood syndromes causing palpitations and anxiety. Some are also used for Deficient Liver *yin* – they tend to be gentle remedies with few side effects.

Sour date seed

Chinese name *Suan zao ren*

Botanical name *Zizi phus jujuba* var. *spinosa*

Taste Sweet, sour

Character Neutral

Meridians Heart, Spleen, Liver, Gall Bladder

Actions Sedative, analgesic, hypotensive, lowers body temperature

Sour date seed

As well as nourishing the Heart, *suan zao ren* is used to combat abnormal sweating, including night sweats. It is sedating and tranquillizing and eases insomnia, palpitations and irritability.

Applications *Suan zao ren* is combined with *fu ling* (tuckahoe) and *chuan xiong* (Szechuan lovage) in *suan zao ren tang* (sour date decoction) to calm the mind and clear Heat.

⊗ Avoid in cases of pathogenic Fire.

Other substances that nourish the Heart and calm the Spirit

- **Mimosa bark** *(he huan pi; Albizzi a julibrissin)*: used for insomnia and irritability but also to invigorate Blood.

- **Chinese senega root** *(yuan zhi; Polygala tenuifolia)*: used to improve the flow of Heart *qi* and clear Phlegm from the Lungs and orifices of the Heart.

FU ZHENG THERAPY

Fu zheng therapy – from *fu*, to strengthen, and *zheng*, constitution – means to restore normality and balance and has been compared with modern Western immunotherapy. The aim is not to treat a specific disease or infection but to strengthen the body as a whole, so that innate resistance and energy can overcome the problem.

Fu zheng can help to increase resistance to disease, prevent tissue damage, destroy abnormal cells, and regulate body functions with allergies, lethargy, repeated infection and slow wound healing all signs of lowered immunity.

Reishi mushroom

In recent *years* the *fu zheng* approach has gained in popularity as an alternative therapy for cancer treatments or to combat AIDS. Research into many of the traditional *fu zheng* plants has highlighted their anti-tumour and immuno-stimulating activity. Patent remedies combining *fu zheng* herbs are now readily available. The list of *fu zheng* herbs includes *huang qi* (milk vetch root), *wu wei zi* (schizandra), *nu zhen zi* (glossy privet berries), *gan cao* (liquorice root); *dang shen* (bellflower root), *bai zhu* (white atractylodes), shiitake mushrooms, seaweeds and Siberian ginseng.

Reishi mushroom

Chinese name *Ling zhi*

Botanical name *Ganoderma lucidem*

Taste Sweet

Character Slightly warm

Meridians Lung, Heart, Spleen, Liver, Kidney

Actions Antiviral, immune stimulant, expectorant, antitussive, antihistamine, antitumour, reduces blood pressure and cholesterol levels

Reishi is the Japanese name for this Oriental bracket fungus that was revered by the ancient Taoists as a longevity tonic. The fungus is used to tonify *qi* and Blood, and also calms the Heart and Spirit. It is traditionally said to encourage determination to live a virtuous life.

Applications *ling zhi* is taken by itself rather than in combination with other herbs – although extracts are now included in many patent *fu zheng* remedies. It can be eaten like other mushrooms in cooking or made into syrups, tinctures or powders, and is used to stimulate the immune system in both general debility and chronic conditions, including cancer.

It is also used for lung problems (including asthma and chronic bronchitis), Heart disharmonies where symptoms include insomnia, palpitations, forgetfulness and hypertension, chronic fatigue syndrome, ME and AIDS.

⊗ Avoid if there are no signs of weakness or Deficiency.

A reishi mushroom infusion

USING HERBAL REMEDIES

Any patient consulting a traditional Chinese medicine practitioner will very likely be sent home with bags of dried herbs to be turned into the daily *tang* (see also page 110). The mixture will probably be based on a centuries-old formula memorized by Chinese medical students and its choice will have been determined by careful diagnosis.

WIDESPREAD AVAILABILITY

Increasingly, Chinese herbs are found in various forms in health food stores, Western pharmacies and on the Internet. A number of these over-the-counter remedies are exact copies of traditional prescriptions, while others may be adapted to remove the less acceptable ingredients. Some are simply single herbs sold as tinctures or powders.

Very few Chinese herbs are taken as single remedies in traditional therapy – the emphasis is always on combinations and how the remedies work together.

Most Chinese herbs sold singly in Western health food shops tend to be tonic remedies and are largely promoted as remedies to combat fatigue, exhaustion or to stimulate the immune system. You will find a table of the most common examples on the opposite page.

Drinking the traditional tang *is often inconvenient for Westerners who prefer pills or tinctures.*

Common Single-herb remedies

- **Dang gui** (Chinese angelica root): May be marketed as dong quai, dong qwai, tang kwai, or Chinese angelica.

- **Dang shen** (bellflower root): Often sold as codonopsis.

- **Dong chong xia cao** (caterpillar fungus): Also sold as cordyceps.

- **Gou qi zi** (wolfberry fruit): Also sold as lycium fruit or goji berries.

- **He shou wu** (fleeceflower root): Also sold as fo ti.

- **Huang qi** (milk vetch root): Often sold as astragalus.

- **Ling zhi** (reishi mushroom): Sold as reishi.

- **San qi** (notoginseng or pseudoginseng root): Sold as san qi ginseng or tian qi.

- **Shi di huang** (prepared Chinese foxglove root) and sheng di huang (fresh or dried Chinese foxglove root): May simply be sold as rehmannia root without any indication of which form has been used. As these two forms of the herb have very different uses care is needed when buying the remedy to be sure the correct one is selected.

- **Ren shen** (Korean ginseng root): May also be sold simply as ginseng, or as Chinese ginseng or red ginseng.

- **Xi yang shen** (American ginseng root): Unlike ren shen, a very yang herb, American ginseng is cooling, supports yin and helps to generate Fluids. It is especially used to nourish Lung yin.

- **Wu jia pi** (Siberian ginseng root bark): The whole root is likely to be used in Western products labelled Siberian ginseng rather than simply the bark as is used in Chinese medicine. Siberian ginseng is largely used by Western herbalists as a remedy to combat stress and jet lag.

- **Wu wei zi** (schizandra fruits): Also sold as Schisandra.

INDEX

PICTURE CREDITS

Special photography: © Octopus Publishing Group/ Ruth Jenkinson; **akg-images**/British Library 30. **Alamy**/ amana images inc./DAJ 113 (t); /Arco Images/O. Diez 147; /Bildagentu r-online 153 (b); Bon Appetit/Ottmar Diez 145; /Bon Appetit /Ian Garlick 123; /Bon Appetit/ Peter Rees 142 (t); /Bon Appetit /Teubner Foodfoto 150; /Flowerphotos/Carol Sharp 148; /Geoffrey Kidd 127, 159; /IMAGEMORE Co., Ltd. 113 (b), 139; /Mary Evans Picture Library 68; /OJO Images Ltd/Sam Edwards 61; / Shoosh/Form Advertising 31; /TH Foto-Werbung /PHOTOTAKE 135. **Bridgeman Art Library**/Archives Charmet 17. **Corbis**/amanaimages /Yasuno Sakata 29; /Blend Images/REB Images 40; /Bloomimage 27; /epa/Jack Bow 78; /Randy Faris 105; /Image Source 64; /Michael A. Keller 90; /PhotoAlto Michele Constantini 57; /PhotoAlto/ Vincent Hazat 82; /Redlink/ Chan Yat Nin 76; /Science Photo Library /Adam Gault 94; /Tetra Images/Jamie Grill 38. **Dorling Kindersley** 115; /Neil Fletcher & Matthew Ward 128; /Steve Gorton 154 (t). **Fotolia**/Arik 51; /Norman Chan 162; /Thierry Hoarau 114. **Garden World Images**/ Gilles Delacroix 117, 146. **Getty Images** 9; /altrendo images 43; /A. Chederros 86; /China Tourism Press 49; /EIGHTFISH 10, 41; /Neil Fletcher & Matthew Ward 129; /Steve Gorton 120, 142 (b); /Jack Hollingsworth 23; /Jose Luis Pelaez Inc. 97; / Frank Lukasseck 52; /PM Images 67; /Benjamin Rondel 28; /Jochen Schlenker 54; / Stockbyte 59, 99; /Keren Su 44, 153; /Dougal Waters 37; / WP Simon 39; /ZenShui/Eric Audras 34. **Octopus Publishing Group**/Stephen Conroy 63; /Mike Hemsley 124, 133, 137, 138, 153, 156, 157, 164, 165. **Photolibrary**/Botanica 168; /Botanica/Heather Weston 167; /BSIP Medical/Chassnet Chassnet 100; /Creatas 80; /Garden Picture Library/ Francois De Heel 107; /imagebroker.net/Bao Bao 119, 130 (b), 140; /JTB Photo 46; /Oxford Scientific (OSF)/ Geoff Kidd 144; /PhotoAlto/ Michele Constantini 102, 170; /Ticket/Ben Pipe 21. **Rex Features**/Garo/Phanie 93. **Wellcome Library, London** 7, 47, 84, 111. **Shutterstock**/ marilyn barbone 130, 132; / Andreja Donko 50; /Dutourdumonde Photography 55; / Image Point Fr 83; /Dimitry Kalinovsky 74; /Kzenon 19; / lightwavemedia 81; /Jasenka Luksa 13; /Monkey Business Images 89; /pavelgr 14; / Quang Ho 116; /successo images 169; /wong sze yuen 18; Yellowj 42; /Eva Ziskova, 12. **Thinkstock**/bedo 134; / marilyna 121, 122, 136, 158; / ribeiroantonio 145.